from Q to "Secret" Mark

A Composition History of the Earliest Narrative Theology

HUGH M. HUMPHREY

t&t clark

NEW YORK • LONDON

Copyright © 2006 by Hugh M. Humphrey

All rights reserved. No part of this book may be reproduced, stored in a retrieval system, or transmitted in any form or by any means, electronic, mechanical, including photocopying, recording, or otherwise, without the written permission of the publisher, T & T Clark International.

T & T Clark International, 80 Maiden Lane, New York, NY 10038

T & T Clark International, The Tower Building, 11 York Road, London SE1 7NX

T & T Clark International is a Continuum imprint.

Cover design: Lee Singer

Library of Congress Cataloging-in-Publication Data
Humphrey, Hugh.
   From Q to secret Mark: a composition history of the earliest narrative theology / Hugh Humphrey.
     p. cm.
   Includes bibliographical references and index.
   ISBN 0-567-02502-0 (hardcover : alk. paper) – ISBN 0-567-02512-8 (pbk. : alk paper)
   1. Bible. N.T. Mark – Criticism, Redaction. 2. Bible. N.T. Mark – Criticism, Narrative. 3. Q hypothesis (Synoptics criticism) 4. Narrative theology. I. Title.
BS2585.52.H84 2006
226.3′066 – dc22

                                                                                               2006001133

Printed in the United States of America
06 07 08 09 10   10 9 8 7 6 5 4 3 2 1

Contents

Acknowledgments	v
Introduction The Focus of This Study	1
Chapter One Revisiting the Fathers	9
Chapter Two A Narrative Version of "Q"	39
Chapter Three The Passion Narrative in Mark	89
Chapter Four Assimilation and a Focus on Discipleship	117
Chapter Five The Composition History of the Gospel of Mark	139
Appendix 1 The "Mark without Q" Hypothesis	149
Appendix 2 Assessing the Quest for a Proto-Mark	155
Index	163

Acknowledgments

It was easier to write this book than it is to acknowledge and thank all who have in diverse ways helped bring it about. Throughout it all, my wife, Ellen, has been an enabler through her steadfast love and loyalty, support and patience. Fairfield University too must be remembered for a sabbatical leave that lead to the initial draft and analysis of the text of the Gospel of Mark. The Catholic Biblical Association' Task Force on the Gospel of Mark offered many helpful suggestions for which I am very grateful. And the editors at T&T Clark have most certainly made me appear to be a better writer. Probably, however, the person I most remember here is the late Monsignor Myles Bourke, whose careful attention to the text of the New Testament in its context set an example for all his students. To these and all others I should have named: I hope this book is a worthy "thank you."

Introduction

The Focus of This Study

It took almost two millennia for the Gospel of Mark to find an audience attentive to and appreciative of its distinctiveness.[1] In the last century and a half, however, biblical scholarship has tried to make up for that neglect with an intense focus on Mark, using a variety of approaches or lenses through which to view this Gospel. Today we are the heirs to that history, and it is only now possible for us to appreciate the unique contribution of the evangelist we call "Mark."

Looking Back

The relatively modern interest[2] in Mark began with the suggestion that it might have been, at least in part, the source for the other Synoptic Gospels of Matthew and Luke; in an era enamored of the new discipline of history, this idea seemed to promise that Mark would be a source closer to the historical Jesus. The hope that one could find in Mark the unadulterated report of Jesus' life was soon tempered, however, by the realization that this Gospel had some materials in it that, to a rational mind, were more mythological than a historical account would be, and by the realization that Mark, too, seemed to have used source materials. Indeed, as the excitement over the actual text of Mark being the lens through which to view the historical Jesus ebbed, it was replaced by the excitement over the analysis of those units of traditional material that had been compiled by the evangelist; this quest to break apart the text of Mark in order to examine and classify those traditional materials

---

1. For an account of the general lack of interest in Mark for most of those two thousand years, see B. D. Schildgen, *Power and Prejudice: The Reception of the Gospel of Mark* (Detroit: Wayne State University Press, 1999), 201.
2. For a thorough review of "how we reached the point where we now are in Marcan studies," see S. P. Kealy, *Mark's Gospel, A History of Its Interpretation: From the Beginning until 1979* (New York: Paulist Press, 1982).

according to their "forms" was still driven by the same hunger to objectively reconstruct the actual history of Jesus. What was characteristic of this development of "form criticism"[3] in Markan studies was fragmentation: small units of the text of the Gospel were studied and compared with other small units of the text of the Gospel; the Gospel as a whole was considered to be the artificial result of a scissors-and-paste editor and therefore to be of no real importance in the quest for the historical Jesus. For some three decades in the first half of the twentieth century, this approach was *the* approach to take in studying Mark, and it did shape the appraisal of Mark in fundamental ways: never again would biblical scholarship be ready to take the Second Gospel as an eyewitness account or a highly reliable historical account: it contained traditional materials.

Perhaps it was the inconsistencies of approach[4] or the questionable assumptions made about the early Christian church that prompted the desire to find a new, objectively verifiable approach to the Gospels that one could defend before all comers. In any event, scholars coupled the intuition that Mark had compiled traditions with the earlier recognition of Matthew and Luke as having compiled Mark and a collection of Jesus' sayings[5] into their Gospels; all this led to development of yet a third approach. Called "redaction criticism" because it studied the precise ways in which Matthew and Luke edited or "redacted" Mark into their Gospels, it was not immediately seen as applicable to the Gospel of Mark. But compilation and redaction are both literary processes; and just as one could now argue for Matthew having an editorial purpose on the basis of how he handled the material in his copy of the Gospel of Mark,[6] so too one could argue for Mark having an editorial purpose on the basis of how he created the "framework" for the units of traditional material and on the basis of the recurring motifs in the Gospel. Again there was fragmentation of the whole text as scholars assembled

---

3. For a concise summary, see Christopher Tuckett, *Reading the New Testament: Methods of Interpretation* (Philadelphia: Fortress, 1987), 95–112.

4. Some judgments were made on the basis of content rather than on the basis of form. For a balanced evaluation see E. Earle Ellis, *The Making of the New Testament Documents* (Biblical Interpretation Series; Leiden: Brill, 1999), 19–23.

5. This collection of sayings of Jesus is commonly referred to as "Q," abbreviating the German word *Quelle* (source). The renewed discussion of the very existence of such a collection will be reviewed later in this introduction and evaluated at the beginning of chapter 2.

6. Whether Matthew had a written or oral copy of the Gospel of Mark is a matter left open here.

individual phrasings and passages to indicate a "motif" or "theme" or "theological interest" of the redactor, in this case, Mark.

This last development of redaction criticism opened the floodgates of biblical scholarship, first and primarily for the study of the Gospels of Matthew and Luke, and then later for Mark; the outpouring of studies continued into the waning years of the last millennium. What is more significant, however, are the other approaches spawned by redaction criticism, each in its own way intrigued by redaction criticism's acknowledgement of the evangelist as a true author speaking theological truths to his community. Let thumbnail sketches suffice.

On the one hand, if we were to position the evangelist as a real author in a concrete, historical situation, an effort to reconstruct the social world of the evangelist was thought to offer new understanding of the nuances of his[7] text; others had undertaken this work in the past, but now it was renewed. For it to be fully effective, one had to make certain assumptions or conclusions about the probable geographical origin of the Gospel's text. Still, general recognition of the distinctive cultural fabric of the Mediterranean basin sharpened our sense of distance from the realities of the first-century cultural world of the evangelists.

Then, too, if we were to think of the evangelist as a person embedded in a social context, then it would be conceivable that models taken from today's social sciences (anthropology, sociology, and so on) could be applied to the information furnished by a Gospel's text and new insights provided thereby. Yet the results depended upon the availability of data, the accuracy of the data, and the trustworthiness of the social science model used.

On the other hand, if we were to emphasize the role of the evangelist as an author, then we could apply the canons of contemporary literary criticism. We could make distinctions between the author implied by the text of the Gospel and the real author; similarly, we could make distinctions between the reader envisioned by the text and the real reader of the first-century Mediterranean world, who in turn would not be the real reader today, with our historical and cultural baggage. Indeed, if we focused upon reader-response criticism, we could detach ourselves from the inadequacy of historical, contextual information — and even from an interest in what the original evangelist's "intention" might have been!

---

7. I would leave open as unestablished the actual gender of any of the evangelists. Use of the male pronoun here is for convenience' sake.

Yet, just as a real community of hearers or readers had originally been the focus of the evangelist's work, so too was there a real author who had produced a text. We could study that Gospel text in and of itself — again abandoning any interest in what the original evangelist's "intention" might have been. And so we have noticed that the Gospel was a story and as such deserved attention to its structure and characterization of the persons within the story and comparison with other stories. Story criticism[8] recentered attention upon the text and away from the uniqueness of each reader's response.

The development called narrative criticism[9] is the first really integrative approach to the text of a Gospel. It attempts to read the text of a Gospel as we must always read or hear it: from the first verse and sequentially through to the last, observing how we can make assumptions on the basis of what the text has already established, and also how the text anticipates future developments. It seeks an empathy with the first-century hearers or readers by appropriation of the reconstructions of that social world. It is also possible to seek an empathy with contemporary readers of a particular cultural world in the same way.

Finally, one should recognize the attention that rhetorical criticism has lately given to the rhetoric of the Gospel of Mark,[10] to the training received by Hellenistic youth, and more particularly to the techniques they employed to develop the simple *chreia* (useful anecdotes) into expanded and elaborated forms.[11] This approach continues the interests developed above with a particular, sharp focus.

Only with narrative criticism has an approach to the Gospel text sought a comprehensive understanding of an evangelist's work; other approaches were fragmentary, focused on particular elements or motifs or segments of the Gospel. Narrative criticism embraces the text as a whole and completed event that we must understand as such. Might it

---

8. E.g., David Rhoads and Donald Michie, *Mark as Story: An Introduction to the Narrative of a Gospel* (Philadelphia: Fortress, 1982). Note also Terrence W. Tilley, *Story Theology* (preface by Robert McAfee Brown; Theology and Life Series 12; Wilmington, DE: Michael Glazier, 1985).

9. For a concise description see Mark Allan Powell, *What Is Narrative Criticism?* (foreword by Dan O. Via; Guides to Biblical Scholarship: New Testament Series; Minneapolis: Fortress, 1990).

10. P. L. Danove, *Linguistics and Exegesis in the Gospel of Mark: Applications of a Case Frame Analysis* (JSNT Supplement Series 218; Sheffield, UK: Sheffield Academic Press, 2001).

11. M. Moeser, *The Anecdote in Mark, the Classical World, and the Rabbis: A Study of Brief Stories in the Demonax, the Mishnah, and Mark 8:27–10:45* (Journal for the Study of the New Testament Supplement Series 227; Sheffield, UK: Sheffield Academic Press / Continuum, 2002).

be possible to move cautiously from that understanding to a statement of the author's "intention/s"?

And Today

As the new millennium opens, a number of new commentaries or studies of Mark's Gospel embrace the approach of narrative criticism.[12] Today there is an appreciation that we must see Mark's text as a whole and as a literarily complex, theologically sophisticated work that speaks to our time as effectively as it must have when initially offered to its community.

It is not the purpose of this book to be yet another narrative-critical study, but rather to describe the process of composition by which that work came into being. I contend that the literary complexity and theological nuances of the Gospel of Mark did not spring from the pen of the evangelist at a single sitting. The image of the cut-and-paste-editor of form criticism can certainly account for some segments of the Gospel text, but not for its integrity and consistency of vision. Rather, I maintain that the evangelist we call "Mark" composed segments of our present Gospel for different situations, over an extended period of time, perhaps several decades, and that the present text reflects the mature, spiritual reflection of the evangelist on the nature of discipleship.

The usual effort to determine the provenance of the Gospel of Mark is, accordingly, an incorrect objective. Commentators call attention to the translation of Aramaic terms, the Latinisms found in the text, the *quadrans* (coin) of Mark 12:42 (Latin Vulgate), the references to persecution in Mark 13 — and then try to determine a *single* place of origin (e.g., Rome[13] or Caesarea[14]). Their judgments on where the Gospel of Mark originated have to remain tentative, since one would need to emphasize some of these pieces of evidence and minimize others. If, as argued here, the composition of the Gospel and hence its provenance occurred over time and in several different situations, then the most that one can determine is the probable place of the final publication of the completed work.

---

12. Thus, e. g., F. J. Moloney, *The Gospel of Mark: A Commentary* (Peabody, MA: Hendrickson, 2002), 398.

13. Cf., e.g., the evaluation by Ray Brown that "Rome as the site cannot be quickly dismissed as implausible," in Raymond E. Brown and John P. Meier, *Antioch and Rome: New Testament Cradles of Catholic Christianity* (New York: Paulist Press, 1983), 191–97.

14. Thus, E. Earle Ellis, *The Making of the New Testament Documents* (Biblical Interpretation Series; Leiden: Brill, 1999), 375.

To establish my thesis concerning the manner in which the Gospel of Mark was composed, I review first the patristic witness to the Gospel of Mark, identifying ambiguities and tensions among them. I give particular emphasis to the witness of Clement of Alexandria, who specifically indicates that Mark wrote several different works. Then in two separate chapters I describe two major segments of Mark — separate compositions, really; it is clear, I argue, that there was a narrative version of the "Q" tradition, the collection of Jesus' sayings[15] that has been viewed as an oral tradition, although a reassessment of it as a "text" has been called for;[16] it is also clear that there was a so-called Passion Narrative. A third development occurs when those two are blended and an emphasis upon discipleship is interwoven into the text, an emphasis particularly colored by the exigencies of the Neronian persecution in Rome in the middle sixties of the first century. With the addition of some explanatory glosses to this last stage of development, the Gospel we call Mark's was complete and received widespread circulation.

I am not reviewing this history of the composition of Mark's Gospel for the purposes of returning to a fragmentary approach or to a renewed interest in Mark's "sources." There have been such efforts. Both Marie-Émile Boismard[17] and Delbert Burkett[18] have recently sought to reconstruct a "Proto-Mark," an earlier source or basis for our present text of the Gospel of Mark. Their approaches differ, and their resulting texts of "Proto-Mark" are, not surprisingly, also different. On the surface it appears that Boismard's position anticipates the position I take here. In fact it does not. While Boismard envisions three components to our present text of Mark's Gospel — a Proto-Mark, a redaction by an editor employing Lukan interests and style, and a passion narrative — there is little overlap between his position and mine, principally because

---

15. That this collection of largely sayings material existed is, plainly, hypothetical since no physical manuscript of it actually exists. That it did exist in some stable form is the contention of the Two-Document Hypothesis, according to which Mark's Gospel and "Q" were the sources used independently by Matthew and Luke. Burnett H. Streeter gave the hypothesis its classic expression in *The Four Gospels* (London: Macmillan, 1924), and this statement of synoptic relationships has been generally accepted as a basis for much subsequent scholarship. A serious challenge to the Q hypothesis has been made, however, by Mark S. Goodacre in *The Case against Q: Studies in Markan Priority and the Synoptic Problem* (Harrisburg, Pa: Trinity Press International, 2002). I evaluate that challenge at the beginning of chapter 2.

16. R. A. Horsley and J. A. Draper, *Whoever Hears You Hears Me: Prophets, Performance, and Tradition in Q* (Harrisburg, PA: Trinity Press International, 1999).

17. M.-É. Boismard, *L'Évangile de Marc: Sa préhistoire* (ÉBib, n.s., 26; Paris: Gabalda, 1994).

18. Delbert Burkett, *Rethinking the Gospel Sources. From Proto-Mark to Mark* (New York: T&T Clark, 2004).

my approach differs so markedly. Boismard employs a careful analysis of the text of Mark and its parallels in Matthew and Luke, seeking to identify the source documents behind our present text of Mark. I focus instead upon the distinguishing narrative interests that disclose first the ultimate righteous teacher of God's kingdom (Son of God), second the suffering Christ, and third the lessons for discipleship when these are combined. In my view, the Gospel of Mark results not from the editing of unattested documents by an unknown redactor for unspecified purpose(s),[19] but from the ever-maturing theological reflection of the Christian tradition's first evangelist, Mark.

Thus, I emphasize I am doing this study for two purposes. If "theology" first of all is the process of bringing faith to expression, then the composition history of Mark's Gospel illustrates that process. Each stage of composition expresses an aspect of the early Christian faith in response to God's having raised Jesus from the dead. The process of theology traced here takes narrative forms. Then, second, this reconstruction of the composition of Mark's Gospel serves to highlight the talent and depth and personality of its author as well as to recognize that the handling of traditions about Jesus in this way provides a useful paradigm for the contemporary church. It is time, today, to appreciate the work of the evangelist we call Mark more fully.

---

19. For more discussion of the Proto-Mark Hypothesis, see appendix 2.

Chapter One

Revisiting the Fathers

*Toward a History of the Composition
of Mark's Gospel*

The internal evidence of the text of Mark's Gospel makes two things clear: (1) Our present text has undergone at least one stage of redaction, when the redactor explained Jewish customs and Aramaic phrasings for an audience apparently unable to understand them.[1] (2) Other stages of redaction have occurred,[2] either in conjunction with that stage of clarification just mentioned or separately. Hence, the various testimonies of the church fathers are most interesting because some of them also either refer to or imply in diverse ways that there were stages of composition in the history of Mark's Gospel. When former scholars reviewed those patristic witnesses, however, they assumed that those references to "Mark" were to our present, canonical text. Accordingly, the testimonies of the early church fathers were confusing: the author could not have written the same text of "Mark" both in Egypt and in Rome, independently of Peter and dependent upon Peter's preaching, with the disinterested knowledge of Peter and with his authoritative approval. If we understand those same testimonies, however, to refer to various stages while writers were composing our present, canonical text, as my analysis of the text of the Gospel has indicated and as I show here, then many of those inconsistencies simply disappear.

Now let's see what the Fathers say.[3]

---

1. Cf. Mark 3:17; 5:41; 7:2–3, 11, 34; 15:22, 34, 42.
2. There are intrusive elements in the present text of Mark, which if omitted would permit the narrative to continue smoothly; cf. esp. Mark 6:14–29; 12:41–44; 14:3–9.
3. In determining the date and place of origin of the Gospel of Mark, "the patristic witnesses — primarily Papias, Irenaeus, Clement, and the Old Latin Prologue — offer the most important evidence, but they are subject to different interpretations," says E. Earle Ellis, "The Date and Provenance of Mark's Gospel," in *The Four Gospels 1992: Festschrift Frans*

The Witness of the Early Church Fathers

Papias

The earliest and most frequently cited reference is in Eusebius's *Ecclesiastical History* 3.39, where he cites the testimony of Papias,[4] who in turn is quoting "the Elder." Papias's testimony, even though reported secondhand, links us back to the middle of the second century; scholars think he was born before the end of the first century and wrote this in his *Exegesis of the Lord's Oracles* about 140 CE.[5] While this time frame appears to distance Papias, Eusebius writes that "Papias himself, according to the preface of his treatises, makes plain that he had in no way been a hearer and eyewitness of the sacred Apostles, but teaches that *he had received the articles of faith from those who had known them*" (emphasis added).[6]

Accordingly, Papias was conscious of his having been but *one* generation removed from the apostolic witness, in this case, that of "the Elder."[7]

The arguments made below will depend upon the Greek text, since, as the following translations show, the passage has been variously interpreted:

καὶ τοῦθ' ὁ πρεσβύτερος ἔλεγεν· Μάρκος μὲν ἑρμηνευτὴς Πέτρου γενόμενος, ὅσα ἐμνημόνευσεν, ἀκριβῶς ἔγραψεν, οὐ μέντοι τάξει, τὰ ὑπὸ τοῦ κυρίου ἢ λεχθέντα ἢ πραχθέντα. οὔτε γὰρ ἤκουσεν τοῦ κυρίου, οὔτε παρηκολούθησεν αὐτῷ, ὕστερον δέ, ὡς ἔφην, Πέτρῳ, ὃς πρὸς τὰς χρείας ἐποιεῖτο τὰς διδασκαλίας, ἀλλ' οὐχ ὥσπερ σύνταξιν τῶν κυριακῶν ποιούμενος λογίων, ὥστε οὐδὲν ἥμαρτεν Μάρκος, οὕτως ἔνια γράψας ὡς ἀπεμνημόνευσεν. ἑνὸς γὰρ ἐποιήσατο πρόνοιαν, τοῦ

Neirynck (ed. F. van Segbroeck et al.; Bibliotheca ephemeridum theologicarum lovaniensium 100; Louvain: Leuven University Press, 1992), 801.

4. For a judicious appraisal, see C. Clifton Black, *Mark: Images of an Apostolic Interpreter* (Columbia, SC: University of South Carolina Press, 1994), 82-94. For a complete citing of the fragments of Papias, see Michael W. Holmes, ed., *The Apostolic Fathers: Greek Texts and English Translations* (Grand Rapids: Baker Books, 1999), 556-95.

5. The dating of Papias's life is uncertain, ranging from a birth in the last third of the first century (65?) to a death in the middle of the second century (163?). The year of 130 for Papias's death seems early, though given by E. Earle Ellis in *The Making of the New Testament Documents* (Biblical Interpretation Series 39; Leiden: Brill, 1999), 358. That date of 130 has also been suggested for Papias's *Exegesis of the Lord's Oracles*.

6. P. Eusebius, *Ecclesiastical History*, vol. 1, *Books 1-5*, and vol. 2, *Books 6-10* (Fathers of the Church 19 and 29; trans. R. J. Deferrari; Washington, DC: Catholic University of America Press, 1953-55), 2.39.2.

7. Thus also C. Clifton Black, *Mark: Images of an Apostolic Interpreter* (Columbia, SC: University of South Carolina Press, 1994), 87.

μηδὲν ὧν ἤκουσεν παραλιπεῖν ἢ ψεύσασθαί τι ἐν αὐτοῖς. Ταῦτα μὲν οὖν ἱστόρηται τῷ Παπίᾳ περὶ τοῦ Μάρκου.

In 1926 Kirsopp Lake translated it thus:

> And the presbyter used to say this, "Mark *became* Peter's interpreter and wrote accurately all that he remembered, not, indeed, in order, of the things said or done by the Lord. For he had not heard the Lord, nor had he followed him, but later on, as I said, followed Peter, who used to give teaching as necessity demanded but not making, as it were, an arrangement of the Lord's oracles, so that Mark did nothing wrong in thus writing down single points as he remembered them. For to one thing he gave attention, to leave out nothing of what he had heard and to make no false statements in them.[8]

Vincent Taylor in 1966 chose this wording:

> And the Elder said this also: Mark, *having become* the interpreter of Peter, wrote down accurately all that he remembered of the things said and done by the Lord, but not however in order. For neither did he hear the Lord, nor did he follow Him, but afterwards, as I said, Peter, who adapted his teachings to the needs *of the hearers*, but not as though he were drawing up a connected account of the Lord's oracles. So then Mark made no mistake in thus recording *some* things just as he remembered them, for he made it his one care to omit nothing that he had heard and to make no false statement therein.[9]

Ralph Martin offered this translation in 1972:

> The Elder said this also: Mark *who has been* Peter's interpreter wrote down carefully as much as he remembered, recording both sayings and doings of *Christ*, not however in order. For he was not a hearer of the Lord, nor a follower, but later a follower of Peter, as I said. And he adapted his teaching to the needs *of his hearers* but

---

8. K. Lake, "Introduction: The Life and Writings of Eusebius," in Eusebius, *The Ecclesiastical History: With an English Translation* (trans. K. Lake; Loeb Classical Library; Cambridge, MA: Harvard University Press, 1926), 291. Emphasis added.

9. V. Taylor, *The Gospel According to St. Mark: The Greek Text with Introduction, Notes, and Indexes* (2d ed.; New York: Macmillan, 1966), 2. Emphasis added. Taylor, too, supplies "of the hearers" and chooses a particular sense of the Greek for his use of "some."

not as one who is engaged in making a compendium of the Lord's precepts.[10]

Most recently E. Earle Ellis made this translation:

> Mark, having become the interpreter of Peter (ἑρμενευτὴς Πέτρου γενόμενος), ... wrote (ἔγραψεν) accurately [in his Gospel], but not indeed in order, the things said or done by the Lord. ... [Peter] used to give his teachings with reference to the [transmitted Gospel] episodes (πρὸς τὰς χρείας) but not, as it were, making an orderly arrangement of the Lord's teachings (λογίων). So Mark did no wrong in thus writing some of the teaching (ἔνια) as he remembered them.[11]

The arguments made below depend upon the Greek text, about which I must make several points:

1. Much depends upon the interpretation one gives to the phrase ἑρμηνευτὴς Πέτρου γενόμενος. One wonders whether to translate it as "Mark *became Peter's interpreter* and wrote..." (Lake); or as "Mark, *having become the interpreter of Peter*, wrote..." (Taylor and Ellis); or as "Mark, *who has been Peter's interpreter*, wrote..." (Martin). To show the ambiguity as sharply as possible, the choices seem to be that Mark (a) "wrote" *after* having become Peter's interpreter (Lake and Taylor) or (b) "wrote" *before* becoming Peter's interpreter, with the phrase in question being simply an identifying comment and properly translated "who became Peter's interpreter," meaning "later" (cf. the ὕστερον, "a short while later").[12]

The correct interpretation of this phrase depends, in turn, upon the judgment one makes about the antecedent for the ὅς. We could understand this relative pronoun to refer back to Mark, but it appears to refer back to the immediately preceding "Peter." That then avoids the awkward repetition of "Peter" and serves to contrast the activity of Peter

---

10. R. Martin, *Mark, Evangelist and Theologian* (Contemporary Evangelical Perspectives; Grand Rapids: Zondervan, 1973), 52. Emphasis added. Martin refers to "Christ" and gratuitously adds "of his hearers." He also chooses not to treat Eusebius's complete reference.
11. Ellis, *Making of the NT Documents*, 358.
12. It is Martin's *translation* that is in focus here. If one sets off the clause "who has been Peter's interpreter" with commas so that it can be understood as an identifying comment and then emphasizes that Mark had been "*later* a follower of Peter," the result is a sense that Mark wrote before he followed Peter. Martin himself does not advance this position, as he makes clear in his "Appendix to Chapter III: A Note on Papias' Witness to Mark," in Martin, *Mark, Evangelist*, 80–83. Martin leans in the direction of placing "the writing of the Gospel after the death of Peter rather than in Peter's lifetime" (81).

with that of Mark in what follows; *Peter* spoke ad hoc and incompletely, and we should not fault *Mark* for recording unconnected bits of information. Thus, Peter becomes the source for the items Mark "wrote" *after* "having become" Peter's interpreter.

So while Papias is actually silent about where Mark *first learned* about "the sayings and doings of the Lord," he seems to insist that what Mark "wrote" derives from Peter. The allusions to Peter underscore the correctness of what Mark has done, assuring its orthodoxy, if you will, even if Mark was not a first-generation eyewitness or follower of Jesus, but only "later" of Peter.

2. But just what was it that Mark wrote? Two phrasings are descriptive: τὰ ὑπὸ τοῦ κυρίου ἢ λεχθέντα ἢ πραχθέντα (the things said and done by the Lord), and οὐχ ὥσπερ σύνταξιν τῶν κυριακῶν ποιούμενος λογίων (not as an arrangement/ordered account of the Lord's sayings). Two things are immediately apparent: the reference to Jesus as "Lord" and not as "Christ,"[13] and the absence of any reference to the suffering, death, and resurrection of Jesus (with which one would expect the term "Christ" to be linked).[14] These phrasings certainly do not suggest our present text of Mark's Gospel ("a Passion Narrative with an extended introduction," as Martin Kähler so famously put it in 1892[15]) and seem to refer to something much less extensive, restricted to an account that focuses on what Jesus *said* and *did*.[16]

3. Another comment: the phrase οὐ μέντοι τάξει (but not in order) seems to reflect a concern that what Mark wrote was not in a chronologically connected narrative; the further explanation is given that Peter presented the "teachings" (τὰς διδασκαλίας) as they were needed, and that resulted in Mark's account being "out of order," as it were. Papias's

---

13. Holmes, *The Apostolic Fathers*, 569n7 affirms his preference for "Christ" here, observing that "other mss and editors read *The Lord*." The two further references to κυρίου and κυριακῶν suggest κυρίου "Lord" should be preferred here.

14. One could say that these are implicit in the use of *kyrios*, but then one says the same for the collection of Jesus' sayings known as Q: while Q appears to have had no Passion Narrative, it must have known of Jesus' resurrection for Jesus' sayings to have had such authority that they needed to be collected.

15. Cf. M. Kähler, *The So-Called Historical Jesus and the Historic Biblical Christ* (ed., trans., and introduced by C. E. Braaten; foreword by P. Tillich; Philadelphia: Fortress, 1964), 80n11.

16. Thus, C. Clifton Black: "One may wonder if Papias's description of Mark's composition actually fits the Gospel that came to be attributed to Mark: at least, that document seems to possess a kind of order (if not completeness)." See C. Clifton Black, *Mark: Images of an Apostolic Interpreter* (Columbia, SC: University of South Carolina Press, 1994), 90. And again: "Although the existence of the Second Gospel that came to be canonized may be presumed, nothing in what Papias says of Mark's literary record could lead us confidently to conclude that" (93).

judgment is clear: Mark's account is not as connected as he, Papias, would like it to be. Exactly what sort of "order" Papias wanted to see, however, is not clear. Perhaps his standard was Matthew, who "collected the oracles" (τὰ λόγια συνετάξατο) "in the Hebrew language,"[17] however one is to imagine that "collection" to have been "ordered." Again, however, Papias's comment about Mark seems puzzling if one refers it to the present text of Mark, which has a clear "order": from Galilee to Jerusalem, from public ministry to public humiliation and death, from divine authorization at Jesus' baptism to an angelic proclamation at Jesus' tomb. Why did Papias perceive it differently? Or, was he actually attesting to something *different* from our present text, but also attributable to Mark?

4. And one final remark: nothing in Papias's testimony explicitly links Mark to Rome or proves an explicit temporal framework for whatever it was that Mark "wrote." The reference to Peter only draws a line of relationship between Peter and Mark, providing authority for the latter's "account" (interestingly also not called a "Gospel"), without saying where or when that relationship occurred. Hugh Anderson's judgment is cautious:

> Since on his own testimony Papias was patently eager to uphold the integrity and worth of Mark, possibly in competition with another Gospel, he and the other ancient authorities who followed him in associating Mark with Peter, and so with Rome, could well have been motivated by the desire to "canonize" Mark, at a time when Rome's influence was definitely on the increase.[18]

The preceding review has, accordingly, raised the real probability that Papias was *not* referring to our present, canonical text of Mark, but to a much less extensive account of what "the Lord" *said* and *did*. The absence of a reference to a messianic Christology, the preference for "Lord" as the way to refer to Jesus, and the emphasis upon the "things said by the Lord" and the "sayings of the Lord" — these all seem to point toward an early moment in the transmission of the traditions about Jesus. If Papias wrote this recollection of what the Elder had said and does so about 140 CE, then, assuming thirty years for a generation to have passed (so that it is Papias who speaks and not the Elder), Papias

---

17. Eusebius, *Hist. eccl.* 3.39.16.
18. Hugh Anderson, *The Gospel of Mark* (New Century Bible Commentary; Grand Rapids: Eerdmans, 1976), 28.

might have learned this from the Elder about 110. But to what was the Elder referring? It appears to be an event long past. Do we go back one more generation to about 80, or two generations to about 50? Such speculation can, without being specific, only point to an early context for what Mark "wrote."

The descriptive phrases flagged above, however, suggest a period even earlier than we have speculated about, a time when Q was being compiled and when the *maran atha* expectation was strong (cf. 1 Cor 16:22). In sum, we can derive three points from this Papias testimony: (1) Mark wrote "the things said and done by the Lord" and did so *after* becoming Peter's "interpreter"; (b) it is unlikely that the Elder was referring to our present, canonical Gospel (what Mark wrote is never here called a "Gospel"); and (c) there are no references to where or when this piece of writing was done, but the way it is described suggests a moment quite early in the tradition.

Clement of Alexandria

Clement of Alexandria (b. 150) makes three references to Mark, and possibly a fourth, which I examine separately. Because of Papias calling Mark a "follower" of Peter, the first of these texts to examine is that reported as originally being in Clement's *Hypotyposes* (*Hypotypôseis, Sketches*), a work of which we have only extracts, such as this one, again reported by Eusebius (*Hist. eccl.* 6.14.5–6):

> Τοῦ Πέτρου δημοσίᾳ ἐν Ῥώμῃ κηρύξαντος τὸν λόγον καὶ πνεύματι τὸ εὐαγγέλιον ἐξειπόντος, τοὺς παρόντας, πολλοὺς ὄντας, παρακαλέσαι τὸν Μάρκον, ὡς ἂν ἀκολουθήσαντα αὐτῷ πόρρωθεν καὶ μεμνημένον τῶν λεχθέντων, ἀναγράψαι τὰ εἰρημένα· ποιήσαντα δέ, τὸ εὐαγγέλιον μεταδοῦναι τοῖς δεομένοις αὐτοῦ· ὅπερ ἐπιγνόντα τὸν Πέτρον προτρεπτικῶς μήτε κωλῦσαι μήτε προτρέψασθαι.

[Again, in the same books, Clement gives the tradition of the earliest presbyters, as to the order of the Gospels, in the following manner: The Gospels containing the genealogies, he says were written first. The Gospel according to Mark had this occasion.] As Peter had preached the Word publicly at Rome, and declared the Gospel by the Spirit, many who were present requested that Mark, who had followed him for a long time and remembered his sayings, should write them out. And having composed the Gospel he gave it to those who had requested it. When Peter learned of this, he neither directly forbade nor encouraged it.[19]

To Papias's witness this testimony adds the detail that Mark "had followed [Peter] *for a long time.*" Clement never specifies when and where Mark had begun his association with Peter. He is concerned to explain the "occasion" of the Gospel of Mark, what had ultimately brought it into being: that "occasion" occurred during Peter's preaching in Rome, some time after Mark had first become Peter's "interpreter."

Clement uses a striking parallelism to describe what Peter was doing in Rome, captured by the translation above: "preached the Word publicly" is balanced by "declared the Gospel by the Spirit." Is the parallelism synonymous or antithetical?[20] What did Clement understand to be the content of "the Word" and of "the Gospel"? Were they the same, or different? When Paul writes to the Corinthians in the early 50s, the content of "the gospel" for him was simply the proclamation of Jesus' death and resurrection; the speeches attributed to Peter in Acts 2 and 3 similarly focus on the death and resurrection of Jesus. Much certainly hinges on determining to some extent the approximate time when Peter did this in Rome. The earlier one imagines Peter to be preaching in Rome, the more likely it is that preaching would be a simple proclamation concerning the death and resurrection of Jesus and its spiritual consequences. From this citation alone one cannot fix a time frame for what Mark will set down as the written record of what Peter said. It must be earlier than 65, when tradition affirms Peter to have been martyred at Rome. If one accepts the tradition that Mark died in 62, it must be well before that. And if the argument I make below is persuasive — that this activity at Rome occurred during the rule of Claudius and before his edict in 49 expelling all Jews from Rome, then we indeed have an early time frame, when it would be likely that the content of "the Word" and of "the Gospel" was simply the proclamation of the death and resurrection of Jesus.

Clement here describes the "occasion" for the Gospel according to Mark as the request by many persons who had heard Peter preach "the Word" and wanted a written form of it. While Papias's testimony spoke

---

19. A. C. McGiffert, trans. and ed., "Eusebius: Church History from A.D. 1–324," in *The Nicene and Post-Nicene Fathers of the Christian Church* (Series 2; vol. 1; ed. P. Schaff; Grand Rapids: Eerdmans, 1952), 261.

20. Paul, for example, distinguishes between his simple, first preaching to the Corinthians and the later "wisdom" that he is able to impart to the spiritually "mature" through the "Spirit that is from God" (1 Cor 2:1–13).

of Mark producing an account of "the things the Lord had said and done," Clement speaks of Mark writing down Peter's preaching of "the Word" and of "the Gospel." It is an *assumption* that Papias and Clement refer to the same text. What the content of "the Word" was is entirely undefined in this citation of Clement, and it is striking that Papias did *not* speak of Mark's written account as a "Gospel," whereas Clement does.

Clement adds the comment that "when Peter discovered this, he neither energetically prevented it nor urged it on," thus suggesting that Peter might have been prompted to "energetically" prevent it for some reason. Was it because what Mark wrote down had material in it unfavorable to Peter, at least on the surface, such as, for example, the account of his denials of Jesus during the passion?

With these comments I propose that Clement here refers to a literary work of Mark different from that attested to by Papias. Papias says Mark wrote an accurate account of what *the Lord* said and did; Clement says Mark wrote a privately circulated account of what *Peter* said, which was the "occasion" for the "Gospel according to Mark." The descriptive phrasings of Papias and of Clement in their respective testimonies suggest a different content for these literary products of Mark. The references to "declared the gospel," which in the 50s for Paul still meant a proclamation of the death and resurrection of Jesus and its spiritual consequences, and to Peter's coolness toward Mark's writing down what he had said, and when we examine such comments in the light of the tradition attested to by the speeches in the Acts of the Apostles that Peter preached about the death and resurrection of Jesus — all these point in the direction of something close to what is today called the Passion Narrative.

Eusebius also claims the same context of Clement's *Hypotyposes* as the source for further material (*Hist. Eccl.* 2.15.1–2):

οὕτω δὴ οὖν ἐπιδημήσαντος αὐτοῖς τοῦ θείου λόγου, ἡ μὲν τοῦ Σίμωνος ἀπέσβη καὶ παραχρῆμα σὺν καὶ τῷ ἀνδρὶ καταλέλυτο δύναμις.

Τοσοῦτον δ' ἐπέλαμψεν ταῖς τῶν ἀκροατῶν τοῦ Πέτρου διανοίαις εὐσεβείας φέγγος, ὡς μὴ τῇ εἰς ἅπαξ ἱκανῶς ἔχειν ἀρκεῖσθαι ἀκοῇ μηδὲ τῇ ἀγράφῳ τοῦ θείου κηρύγματός διδασκαλίᾳ, παρακλήσεσιν δὲ παντοίαις Μάρκον, οὗ τὸ εὐαγγέλιον φέρεται, ἀκόλουθον ὄντα Πέτρου, λιπαρῆσαι ὡς ἂν καὶ διὰ γραφῆς ὑπόμνημα τῆς διὰ λόγου παραδοθείσης αὐτοῖς καταλείψοι διδασκαλίας, μὴ πρότερόν τε ἀνεῖναι ἢ κατεργάσασθαι τὸν ἄνδρα, καὶ ταύτῃ αἰτίους γενέσθαι τῆς τοῦ λεγομένου κατὰ Μάρκον εὐαγγελίου γραφῆς. γνόντα δὲ τὸ πραχθέν φασι τὸν ἀπόστολον ἀποκαλύψαντος αὐτῷ τοῦ πνεύματος, ἡσθῆναι τῇ τῶν ἀνδρῶν προθυμίᾳ κυρῶσαί τε τὴν γραφὴν εἰς ἔντευξιν ταῖς ἐκκλησίαις.

Κλήμης ἐν ἕκτῳ τῶν Ὑποτυπώσεων παρατέθειται τὴν ἱστορίαν, συνεπιμαρτυρεῖ δὲ αὐτῷ καὶ ὁ Ἱεραπολίτης ἐπίσκοπος ὀνόματι Παπίας.

And thus when the divine word had made its home among them, the power of Simon was quenched and immediately destroyed, together with the man himself. And so greatly did the splendor of piety illumine the minds of Peter's hearers that they were not satisfied with hearing once only, and were not content with the unwritten teaching of the divine Gospel, but with all sorts of entreaties they besought Mark, a follower of Peter, and the one whose Gospel is extant, that he would leave them a written monument of the doctrine which had been orally communicated to them. Nor did they cease until they had prevailed with the man, and had thus become the occasion of the written Gospel which bears the name of Mark. And they say that Peter, when he had learned through a revelation of the Spirit, of that which had been done, was pleased with the zeal of the men, and that the work obtained the sanction of his authority for the purpose of being used in the churches. Clement in the eighth book of his *Hypotyposes* gives this account, and with him agrees the bishop of Hierapolis named Papias.[21]

However, given the much briefer extract from Clement's *Hypotyposes* cited earlier and its coolness of Peter toward what Mark had written, we do not know how much of this present text should be attributed to Clement. When one looks at the preceding context, it is clearly Eusebius recounting the history of Simon Magus (*Hist. eccl.* 2.13). He speaks about Peter besting Simon Magus, first in Judea, and then following him to Rome to oppose him there as well (2.14). This prompts the longer account of the "occasion" for Mark to provide a written account of Peter's preaching (2.15).

The citation is particularly intriguing.

1. One must consider the likelihood of an extended period between Mark's being "prevailed upon" and the final "Scripture which is called

---

21. McGiffert, "Eusebius," 115–16.

the Gospel according to Mark," since it is difficult to imagine a text as long as our present Gospel of Mark being composed quickly. Perhaps the intent of the phrase "they did not cease until they had prevailed upon the man" is to recognize that Mark began the process of writing down what the oral teaching had been and had to be encouraged to continue on to complete it as a "Gospel."

2. While the citation seems to report the same situation as the previous one, it describes an entirely different formal reaction to what Mark had written down. In this case "the apostle" (in context, Peter) "authorized the Scripture for reading in the churches." It therefore was no longer a privately circulated document. Nevertheless, this is introduced by "they say," which in Eusebius indicates a generally held tradition[22] at the time Eusebius wrote. The preceding material (Peter in Rome, preaching; Mark urged to write) seems to be a paraphrase of Clement's testimony. The information about Peter's reaction may be a tradition in Eusebius's day about "the Scripture which is called the Gospel according to Mark" (the phrase immediately preceding "they say"), a tradition that it was accepted in the church because Peter himself had authorized it. This latter tradition, however, may well refer to the completed text of Mark in Eusebius's day and not to what Mark initially wrote in Rome, which was but the "occasion" for the finished Gospel.

3. Also intriguing is the phrase "to leave (behind) with them," which certainly implies that Mark was known to be about to depart for someplace. In the immediately following passage (*Hist. eccl.* 2.16.1) Eusebius reports a commonly accepted tradition ("they say") that "this Mark was the first to be sent to preach in Egypt the Gospel which he had *also* put into writing, and was the first to establish churches in Alexandria itself." Here Eusebius is not continuing a citation from Clement of Alexandria, whom we could expect to supply such information, but a generally held tradition. Still, Eusebius locates Peter's refutation of Simon Magus during the reign of Claudius (2.14.6), and so for all practical purposes sometime before 49, when Claudius expelled all Jews from Rome. If that is the context for "to leave (behind) with them," then those who are petitioning Mark to write would not themselves have been Jews.

A third passage from the writings of Clement also speaks of this:

---

22. P. Sellew, "Eusebius and the Gospels," in *Eusebius, Christianity, and Judaism* (ed. H. W. Attridge and G. Hata; Detroit: Wayne State University Press, 1992), 117–18.

> Marcus, Petri sectator, praedicante Petro evangelium palam Romae coram quibusdam Caesareanis equitibus et multa Christi testimonia proferente, petitus ab eis, ut possent quae dicebantur memoriae commendare, scripsit ex his, quae Petro dicta sunt, evangelium quod secundum Marcum vocitatur. (*Adumbr. in 1 Pet.* 5:13)

> Mark, the follower of Peter, while Peter was preaching publicly the gospel at Rome in the presence of certain of Caesar's knights and was putting forward many testimonies concerning Christ, being requested by them that they might be able to commit to memory the things which were being spoken, wrote from the things which were spoken by Peter the Gospel which is called according to Mark.[23]

This passage is fundamentally consistent with the previous two. Peter is preaching publicly, and Mark is asked to write down what Peter has said. I have suggested that the content of what Mark wrote at this time may have been an account of Jesus' passion, death, and resurrection. Similarly, Clement states that Peter is "preaching...the *Gospel*," a phrasing balanced by "putting forward many testimonies *concerning Christ*," language consistent with our suggestion. A new detail here, however, is that it was "certain of Caesar's knights" who were one particular audience of Peter's and the ones also who requested that Mark write. Nevertheless, Clement gives no additional comment concerning Peter's reaction to what Mark was doing.

There remains a fourth text attributed to Clement, a fragment of a letter to Theodore, the authenticity of which has been the subject of much scholarly discussion for a variety of reasons. I will, accordingly, put off an examination of it until the end of this review of the undisputed evidence of the early church fathers.

Recap of Papias and Clement

I summarize the evidence thus far:

- Mark, having become a follower of Peter, wrote down both what the Lord had said and what the Lord had done, accurately, though not in order (Papias).

- Mark followed Peter a "long time" (Clement).

---

23. Taylor, *St. Mark*, 6.

Revisiting the Fathers

- When Peter was in Rome, Mark was asked, at the urging of "many," or certain knights of Caesar's, to write down what he remembered Peter preaching, meaning the proclamation of the "gospel" and "testimonies concerning Christ" (Clement).
- When Peter learned what Mark was doing, he neither encouraged nor discouraged it (Clement).
- Mark then left Rome and so too, presumably, did Peter (Clement).
- At some point "the apostle" approved what Mark had written and authorized it to be read in the churches (independent tradition that Eusebius attaches to Clement's testimony).

Conflicting Testimony?

Two texts appear to conflict with the picture advanced by Papias and Clement because in the past readers have understood these texts to assert that Mark did not write his Gospel until *after* Peter died.

1. The second century (c. 160–180) Anti-Marcionite Prologue to Mark's Gospel, in addition to a comment on Mark's nickname as "stump-fingered," reports:

   iste interpres fuit Petri, post excessionem ipsius Petri descripsit idem hoc in partibus Italiae evangelium.

   He was the interpreter of Peter. After the death of Peter himself he wrote down this same gospel in the regions of Italy.[24]

   This early witness is usually the basis for countering the picture given thus far that Mark had written while Peter was still alive. If *post excessionem ipsius Petri* is translated, as most do, "after the death of Peter himself," then the clear meaning is the exact opposite. But *excessionem* need not have only that sense. As T. W. Manson[25] pointed out, it could refer to Peter's "departure" from Rome after his visit there. In that event the tension with the testimony of Clement disappears, and the gist is entirely the same: after Peter left Rome, Mark wrote what would be called the Gospel according to Mark. Rome is not specifically mentioned as the place

---

24. Ibid., 3.
25. T. W. Manson, *Studies in the Gospels and Epistles* (ed. M. Black; Manchester: Manchester University Press, 1962), 33ff.

where Mark wrote, but *in partibus Italiae* could be understood in that sense.

2. A little later (c. 180–188[26]), Irenaeus (120–202) writes (*Haer.* 3.1.2):

> Μετὰ δὲ τὴν τούτων ἔξοδον Μάρκος, ὁ μαθητὴς καὶ ἑρμηνευτὴς Πέτρου, καὶ αὐτὸς τὰ ὑπὸ Πέτρου κηρυσσόμενα ἐγγράφως ἡμῖν παραδέδωκεν.

> And after the death of these [Peter and Paul] Mark, the disciple and interpreter of Peter, also transmitted to us in writing the things preached by Peter.[27]

Taylor argues that Irenaeus thus agrees with the Anti-Marcionite Prologue and that the natural meaning of the word Irenaeus uses, ἔξοδον, is "as in Luke ix. 31 of departure in the sense of death, thus giving chronological information regarding the date of composition. The reference to Rome (ἐν Ῥώμῃ) in the context implies that the Gospel was composed there."[28]

Perhaps scholars have examined this text through a distorting lens because they did not take it in context. The larger focus of Irenaeus's concern was the establishment of the Christian canon of Scripture on a consistent basis:

> Everything that had been in use in the Christian communities from the beginning was...included, if the tradition of the churches would confirm its use. The concept of apostolicity appears in a modified form: the authors of the writings collected in the canon were, to be sure, either apostles or disciples of apostles — with Paul counting as an apostle; but actually they only expressed what was the real criterion of the canon, namely the teachings of the churches in the earliest period, meaning whichever of these writings had actually remained in use since that time.[29]

That context becomes apparent when the testimony under examination here is placed in its larger context (*Haer.* 3.1).

---

26. D. J. Unger, trans. and ed., *St. Irenaeus of Lyons against the Heresies* (Ancient Christian Writers 55; New York: Paulist Press, 1992), 3–4.
27. Taylor, *St. Mark*, 4.
28. Ibid., 4–5.
29. H. Koester, *History and Literature of Early Christianity* (Introduction to the New Testament; Philadelphia: Fortress, 1982), 10.

> We have learned from none others the plan of our salvation, than from those through whom *the Gospel has come down to us, which they did at one time proclaim in public, and, at a later period, by the will of God, handed down to us in the Scriptures,* to be the ground and pillar of our faith. For it is unlawful to assert that they preached before they possessed "perfect knowledge," as some do even venture to say, boasting themselves as improvers of the apostles. For *after our Lord rose from the dead,* [the apostles] were invested with power from on high when the Holy Spirit came down [upon them], were filled from all [His gifts], and had perfect knowledge; they *departed to the ends of the earth, preaching the glad tidings of the good things [sent] from God to us* and proclaiming the peace of heaven to men, who indeed do all equally and individually possess the Gospel of God. *Matthew also* issued a written Gospel among the Hebrews in their own dialect, while *Peter and Paul* were preaching at Rome, and laying the foundations of the Church. *After their departure, Mark, the disciple and interpreter of Peter did also hand down to us in writing what had been preached by Peter. Luke* also, the companion of Paul, recorded in a book the Gospel preached by him. Afterwards, *John,* the disciple of the Lord, who also had leaned upon His breast, did himself publish a Gospel during his residence at Ephesus in Asia.[30]

In other words, Irenaeus's emphasis is not on when Mark "wrote" his Gospel, but rather on the fact that his Gospel, already in completed form, passes on to us, the next generation, what Peter himself had preached during the apostolic era. Irenaeus is affirming a first-generation, Spirit-filled era in which the gospel of God was preached by Peter and Paul and, in writing, by Matthew (also an apostle), and a second generation linked back to that first generation's witness: Mark, linked to Peter; Luke, to Paul, John, to Jesus himself. We should take the statement about Mark in that larger context; when the apostolic age had closed, with the deaths of Peter and Paul, Mark's Gospel provided a written form of the preaching of Peter, whose disciple Mark was. Interpreted in this manner, the evidence for Mark's having actually written his work after the death of Peter seems less strong because the emphasis is clearly on the verb

---

30. Alexander Roberts and James Donaldson, eds., *Anti-Nicene Fathers,* I. *The Apostolic Fathers, Justin Martyr, Irenaeus* (Peabody, MA: Hendrickson, 1995), 414. Emphasis added.

παραδέδωκεν and not on the adverb "in writing." The emphasis is on the *Gospel,* not the individual named "Mark."

Irenaeus's point is clear. He knows of the four Gospels: Those of Mark, Luke, and John he assigns to the generation of Christian witness that followed upon the first generation of apostolic preaching. He also knows that the church became dependent upon the reliable authority of those second-generation Gospels. But should one give more weight to this testimony of Irenaeus that Mark wrote after the "death" of Peter than to Papias's and Clement's affirmation that Mark wrote while Peter was still alive? Because of the polemical interest and the artificial structure of the larger context, and Irenaeus's casualness in reconstructing historical (as opposed to "theological") tradition, it seems not. Mark of necessity is said to be second-generation ("after the departure" of Peter and Paul) because he was well-known in the tradition to have been "the disciple and interpreter of Peter." Hence, in the second generation Mark's Gospel continues (παραδέδωκεν) to us also (καὶ αὐτὸς) in written form what Peter had preached. What Irenaeus understands by Mark's "writing" must have been something like our established, present text of Mark. Exactly when, however, that written form actually came into being, when Mark "wrote" it, remains an open issue here.

3. It is not certain, therefore, the testimonies of the Anti-Marcionite Prologue and of Irenaeus give us evidence that Mark wrote after the death of Peter. The former may not be speaking of Peter's "death" at all, and Irenaeus seems really to beg the question by focusing instead on Mark's text as a written form of Peter's apostolic preaching for the second and subsequent generations of Christians.

The Egyptian Connection

There is a strong tradition affirming that Mark was in Egypt.[31] For those who hold a monolithic (or should we say "monographic"?) view that Mark wrote his entire Gospel at once, these Egyptian traditions are given less weight because the references to "persecutions" within the Gospel itself and its "Latinisms"[32] appear to provide evidence that Rome was

---

31. C. Wilfred Griggs calls attention to the reference in Acts 18:24 to "Apollos, a native of Alexandria" and to the additional note in the Codex Bezae (D), "He had been instructed in his homeland," as evidence that "Christianity had arrived in Alexandria, at least, by the middle of the first century." He reports a "general consensus that Christianity had to be taken to Egypt by approximately 50 CE and most commentators accept that interpretation." See his *Early Egyptian Christianity from Its Origins to 451 CE* (Boston: Brill, 2000), 16–17.

32. William Lane summarizes the evidence: "In language, Mark shows a distinct preference for Latin technical terms, particularly terms connected with the army (e.g. *legion,* Ch. 5:9;

the appropriate setting for the Gospel's composition. What I suggest here, by contrast, is a developmental understanding of the composition of Mark's Gospel. I will show that the narrative characteristics of the present text provide reasons for asserting layers within the present Gospel, indicating that the Gospel we now have is the synthesis of several stages of composition and written, plausibly, in different locations. This perspective provides a basis for reviewing the "Egyptian tradition" in a less jaundiced, more favorable light.

Eusebius

I have already alluded to the first of Eusebius's two statements associating Mark with Egypt. It is the report of a generally held view (*Hist. eccl.* 2.16.1):

Τοῦτον δὲ Μάρκον πρῶτόν φασιν ἐπὶ τῆς Αἰγύπτου στειλάμενον, τὸ εὐαγγέλιον, ὃ δὴ καὶ συνεγράψατο, κηρῦξαι, ἐκκλησίας τε πρῶτον ἐπ' αὐτῆς Ἀλεξανδρείας συστήσασθαι.³³

They say that this Mark was the first to be sent to preach in Egypt the Gospel which he had also put into writing, and was the first to establish churches in Alexandria itself.³⁴

This text is of particular interest because it provides part of the organizational framework for Eusebius's following development. After placing Mark in Egypt with this comment, he can then report another tradition that "he [Mark] came to Rome in the time of Claudius to speak to Peter, who was at that time preaching to those there."³⁵ This subsequent remark offers a setting for Eusebius to then review Philo's writings (2.17–18). The reference to "Claudius" (in 2.17.1) then provides the setting for a review of Josephus's material on contemporary riots and quarrels (2.19–21), followed by the accounts of Paul's difficulties during the reign of Nero (2.22) and of James's death (2.23), reported by

---

praetorium, Ch. 15:16; *centurion*, Ch. 15:39), the courts (e.g. *speculator*, Ch. 6:27; *flagellare*, Ch. 15:15) and commerce (e.g., *denarius*, Ch. 12:15; *quadrans*, Ch. 12:42). Although such terms were in use throughout the empire, it is particularly significant that twice common Greek expressions in the Gospel are explained by Latin ones (Ch. 12:42, 'two copper coins [*lepta*], which make a *quadrans*'; Ch. 15:16, 'the palace, that is the *praetorium*).'" The presence of Latinisms and of technical terminology confined to the West fits the tradition that Mark was written in Rome.
33. Eusebius, *Hist. eccl.* 2.16.1 (Lake, 144).
34. Ibid., 145.
35. Ibid., 2.17.1 (Lake, 145).

several sources, including Josephus. At that point, Eusebius *returns* to Mark, Nero, and Alexandria (2.24) before beginning an account of the reign of Nero (2.25).

The context for the testimony under review, therefore, indicates that these references to Mark's being in Alexandria in 2.16.1 and 2.25 were part of his stable and accepted set of facts, within which other material could be integrated. Mark's association with Alexandria and Egypt was so well-known that Eusebius took it for granted and used it as the organizing principle for the *Ecclesiastical History* at that point.

With respect to the text cited above, the comment is a peculiar one if one understands it as a reference to our present text of Mark because it is hard to imagine how one could "preach" that entire literary work. Indeed, some parts of our present text are quite difficult to "preach" about: two examples are the healing of the blind man in 8:22–26, where the healing is inefficacious the first time around; and the phrase in 10:18, where Jesus protests being called "good." But passages such as these are not what come to mind when one thinks of "preaching" the "gospel." Rather, one thinks of the passion and death and resurrection of Jesus, of his obedience to the will of God, even to the point of death, for which God rewarded him by exalting him; and of the foolishness of the cross, which discloses the wisdom of God for all humankind, as Paul spoke of it in 1 Cor 1.

What Mark had "put into writing," therefore, was this "gospel" that he also preached. It need not have been the full literary text of our present Gospel, but it must have certainly contained the proclamation of God's having raised Jesus from the dead after Jesus totally gave himself up. It is not clear whether it also contained the compilation of "what Jesus said and did," as mentioned by Papias, including an account of Jesus announcing God's eschatological kingdom. Did early Christianity "preach" that as the "gospel"? When Mark joins the latter with the former, he presents us with "the beginning" (in what Jesus said and did) of the "good news" (God's raising Jesus from the dead after his passion), as Mark describes his literary work at that point, in Mark 1:1.

There is no tension, therefore, between this traditional memory ("they say") associating Mark with Egypt and what has been described by Papias and Clement. Mark began to put the traditions about Jesus into writing. While Peter was preaching in Rome, he continued to write, but this time focused on the "gospel" that Peter "preached." When he left Rome for Egypt, bringing his literary work with him (having left a copy of his account of the passion, death, and resurrection of Jesus behind with those who had asked him to write), he began a period of "preaching" the "gospel" in Egypt independently of Peter. The many references to Mark as the "interpreter" and "disciple" of Peter do not oblige us to believe that Mark had no ministry independent of Peter's; indeed, Papias and Eusebius's testimony point in exactly the other direction.

Eusebius also makes a second reference to Mark's presence in Egypt, as mentioned above (*Hist. eccl.* 2.24):

Νερῶνος δὲ ὄγδοον ἄγοντος τῆς βασιλείας ἔτος, πρῶτος μετὰ Μάρκον τὸν εὐαγγελιστὴν τῆς ἐν Ἀλεξανδρείᾳ παροικίας Ἀννιανὸς τὴν λειτουργίαν διαδέχεται.[36]

In the eighth year of the reign of Nero, Annianus was the first after Mark the Evangelist to receive charge of the diocese of Alexandria.[37]

Without explaining his purpose, Eusebius baldly reports the succession of Annianus to the responsibilities Mark had exercised over the diocese of Alexandria. The reference to "Nero" prepares for the subsequent treatment of Nero's reign, which continues to the end of book 2. While the statement about Annianus's succession does not specifically say that Mark has died, that would be a natural understanding of the circumstance for the change from Mark to Annianus. Such an understanding would also bring closure to the narrative about Mark, which Eusebius has used as a framework for much of book 2. In any event, the change in Mark's ministry is said to occur in the eighth year of Nero's reign, thus in 62.

Jerome (347–420)

This fourth-century scholar and exegete refers to the traditions about Mark in two texts. One of these is in the context of a preface (written in 398) to his *Commentary on Matthew,* where he presents thumbnail sketches of the authors of the Gospels. About Mark he writes:

Secundus Marcus, interpres apostoli Petri et Alexandrinae ecclesiae primus episcopus, qui dominum quidem salvatorem ipse non vidit,

---

36. Ibid., 2.24 (Lake, 178).
37. Ibid., 2.24 (Lake, 179).

sed ea quae magistrum audierat praedicantem, iuxta fidem magis gestorum narravit quam ordinem.[38]

Second, Mark, the interpreter of the Apostle Peter and the first Bishop of the Church of Alexandria, who himself did not see the Lord the Saviour, but narrated those things which he heard his master preaching, with fidelity to the deeds rather than to their order.[39]

As Taylor observes, "The new point is the tradition that Mark was the first bishop of Alexandria. This tradition was not mentioned by Papias, Clement, and Origen." Taylor asserts that it is "impossible to harmonize" this tradition with the testimony of those early Fathers and "the Roman tradition which these writers attest," a position understandable when Taylor wrote but which needs to be reexamined today in light of my thesis.

My interest in Jerome's statements derives from two factors. The first is Jerome's own history. Converted at age 18, he spent a period of time as an ascetical hermit, was ordained in 379, and three years later became secretary to Pope Damasus in Rome. There at age 40 he translated the New Testament into Latin (383). When Damasus died in 384, he left Rome, going first to Antioch and then to Alexandria before settling in Bethlehem (386), where he died on September 30, 420. He had contact, therefore, with both the Roman and Alexandrian churches and their traditions, but when he wrote his preface to the *Commentary on Matthew* in 398, he had already settled in Bethlehem, away from the direct influence of either of those churches. His statement associating Mark with Alexandria is all the more remarkable, therefore, and particularly because the preface was addressed to Eusebius of Cremona, who was himself going to Rome. Jerome's silence about Rome as the place of origin for Mark's Gospel gives a quite deliberate preference to the Alexandrian tradition.

The second reason for an interest in Jerome's remarks, though made in the late fourth century, is precisely that they attest to the continuing and strong tradition associating Mark with Alexandria. That fact alone should prompt us to challenge Taylor's judgment above.

And one more observation: it is certainly a *completed* version of Mark's Gospel to which Jerome refers, since it is listed alongside those

---

38. Jerome, *Commentariorum in Matthaeum*, Prologus, 6.
39. Taylor, *St. Mark*, 7.

of Matthew, Luke, and John; Jerome cannot be understood to refer to something less, something still in the process of being finished. Yet it also is true that his description of that Gospel sounds much like Papias's, which may not be referring to the completed text.

The core of the difficulty comes from the second of the two statements by Jerome, which appears as chapter 8 in his *De viris illustribus*. The work presents succinct descriptions of 135 individuals, ending with Jerome himself. Not all entries are of equal length; much more is said of James the Just (chap. 2) than of Peter (chap. 1), and more of Philo the Jew (chap. 11) than of any of the synoptic evangelists. What Jerome presents, however briefly, he says confidently; it is of interest, therefore, because it represents the history and tradition of the early church as Jerome knew it and could affirm it without fear of contradiction in 392. With respect to Mark he writes:

> Marcus, discipulus et interpres Petri, iuxta quod Petrum referentem audierat, rogatus Romae a fratribus breue scripsit euangelium. Quod cum Petrus audisset, probauit et ecclesiis legendum sua auctoritate edidit, sicut scribunt Clemens in sexto ὑποτυπώσεων libro et Papias Hierapolitanus episcopus. Meminit huius Marci et Petrus in prima epistula sub nomine Babylonis figuraliter Romam significans: Salutat uos quae est in Babylone cumelecta Marcus, filius meus. Adsumpto itaque euangelio quod ipse confecerat, perrexit Aegyptum et primus Alexandriae Christum adnuncians constituit ecclesiam tanta doctrina et uirtute continentiae ut omnes sectatores Christi ad exemplum sui cogeret. Denique Philon, dissertissimus Iudeorum, uidens Alexandriae primam ecclesiam adhuc iudaizantem quasi in laudem gentis suae et super eorum conuersatione scripsit, et quomodo Lucas narrat Hierosolymae credentes omnia habuisse communia, sic ille quod Alexandriae sub Marco fieri doctore cernebat memoriae tradidit. Mortuus est autem octauo Neronis anno et sepultus Alexandriae succedente sibi Anniano.[40]

Mark, the disciple and interpreter of Peter, wrote a short gospel at the request of the brethren at Rome embodying what he had heard Peter tell. When Peter had heard this, he approved it and issued it

---

40. Jerome, *De viris illustribus* (Sammlung ausgewählter kirchen- und dogmengeschichtlicher Quellenschriften; Frankfurt: Minerva, 1968), 12.

to the churches to be read by his authority, as Clement, in the sixth book of his Ὑποτυπώσεις and Papias, bishop of Hierapolis, record.

2. Peter also mentions this Mark in his First Epistle, figuratively indicating Rome under the name of Babylon: "She who is in Babylon, chosen together with you, salutes you; and so does my son Mark."

3. So, taking the *Gospel* which he himself composed, he went to Egypt and, first preaching Christ at Alexandria, he formed a church with such great continence in doctrine and life that he constrained all followers of Christ to his example.

4. Philo, then, most eloquent of the Jews, seeing the first church at Alexandria still following Jewish customs, wrote a book on their manner of life as something creditable to his nation, and, as Luke says that "the believers had all things in common," so he recorded what he saw was done at Alexandria, under the learned Mark.

5. He died in the eighth year of Nero and was buried at Alexandria, leaving Annianus at his successor.[41]

With two notable affirmations, Jerome seems to have drawn the elements of this testimony from the other materials we have already reviewed. That Mark was "the disciple and interpreter of Peter" is clearly derived from the tradition embodied in Papias's reference.

That Mark "wrote ... at the request of the brethren at Rome embodying what he had heard Peter tell" we derive from Eusebius's reporting of Clement's testimony in *Hist. eccl.* 6.24.5–6 and 15.1–2.

That Peter "approved it and published it to the churches to be read by his authority" is drawn from Eusebius's *Hist. eccl.* 15.1–2, but in tension with 6.14.5–6. That Jerome here prefers the text of 15.1–2 is suggested by the continuing reference to Papias in this same context.

The comment that Peter refers to Mark in his First Epistle is a new element, but this may be derived from Jerome's own exegesis of that passage in 1 Peter rather than from traditional information.

Then Jerome returns to Eusebius's *Ecclesiastical History* and comments: "So, taking the Gospel that he himself composed, he went to Egypt and, first preaching Christ at Alexandria, he formed a church"; this echoes *Hist. eccl.* 16.1. He appends a laudatory comment about the

---

41. Thomas P. Halton, trans. *Saint Jerome: On Illustrious Men* (The Fathers of the Church, vol. 100; Washington, DC: Catholic University of America Press, 1999).

Alexandrian church — "so admirable in doctrine and continence of living that he constrained all followers of Christ to his example" — that appears to have been drawn from his own reading of an unspecified book by Philo the Jew, to which he later refers in his chapter on Philo the Jew (*Vir. ill.* 11).

And last, the reference to the "eighth year of Nero, ... Annianus succeeding him" is evidently drawn from *Hist. eccl.* 2.24.

Thus, Jerome's testimony is largely an encyclopedic one, drawn from source materials to compile the information he offers. Yet there are two notable affirmations that apparently cannot be traced back in a similar way to earlier tradition. The first is that Mark wrote "a short Gospel." Is this Jerome's own judgment, knowing as he does in his day the length of the evangelists' completed literary works? Or does he here, also, know of a tradition that we have not yet reviewed?

The second distinctive affirmation is more critical: the reference to the death and burial of Mark at Alexandria in the eighth year of Nero's reign (62 CE). V. Taylor reports the comment by Swete that Jerome's statement "seems to be merely an unsound inference from the Eusebian date for the succession of Annianus." We have reviewed (above) the tradition that Mark wrote *after* Peter had died; this affirmation by Jerome that Mark died in 62 would stand in sharp contrast with that, given the traditional dating of Peter's death as 65. More pointedly, even, is the conflict between Jerome's dating and the modern scholarly tendency to date the composition of Mark to 65, whatever the reasoning used. If Jerome is correct, if the succession of Annianus in 62 is indeed witness to the death of Mark, then the Gospel's composition could not have occurred in 65 but must have occurred considerably earlier.

What we should not overlook is the tandem comment by Jerome that Mark "was buried at Alexandria." An inference of death because of succession is one thing; but the assertion of burial in a named place is far more specific. Places of burial and of monuments marking them are well-known, and Jerome's statement could have been readily and easily challenged if it were known to be untrue. Furthermore, to dismiss Jerome's testimony about the death of Mark as an "unsound inference" is to ignore the care with which Jerome has proceeded in his comments about Mark. Jerome could substantiate all the preceding information by reference to other existing sources. Why should one here impute carelessness to Jerome? Why not take his testimony seriously?

The association of Mark with Egypt in general, and with Alexandria in particular, does not seem to depend simply upon the testimony of Clement, repeated first by Eusebius and subsequently by Jerome. Jerome adds to the traditions of Mark in Egypt an extended remark about Philo's praise of the Alexandrian church established by Mark. Jerome gives no specific title for the "book concerning the first church of Mark the evangelist at Alexandria"[42]; but inasmuch as his approach has been encyclopedic, including materials from existing sources, we should assume that Jerome's testimony is to be trusted and that Philo the Jew did indeed attest in writing to Mark's successful presence in Alexandria.

The very conjunction of the two names "Philo" and "Mark" should give us pause, since Philo Judaeus died in 50 CE, pushing the date for Mark's movement to Egypt back into the 40s of the first century.

Clement of Alexandria and the "Secret Gospel"

There is another testimony attributed to Clement of Alexandria. I have left it until now because scholarly opinion about its authenticity has been divided.[43] Nonetheless, I review it here because of its striking parallel, in some respects, to the reconstruction of the composition history of Mark unfolding in this revisiting of the patristic testimonies and in the earlier analysis of the narrative characteristics of Mark's Gospel. This testimony comes from the discovery of a letter fragment by Clement, reported to the scholarly world[44] and the popular press by Morton Smith. Controversy immediately arose because of Smith's interpretation of the letter and his suggestion that it referred to a "secret" Gospel of Mark, not previously known, and used in connection with secret initiation rituals with (homo)sexual overtones.

Controversy continues to this day, principally because no other scholar in the last quarter century has been able physically to examine the actual letter itself. Although Smith published photographs of it in his 1973 commentary on the letter fragment, the monastic community in whose library

---

42. Ibid., chap. 11.
43. C. Wilfred Griggs's judgment is that "the overwhelming majority of those who had written on the subject believe that the letter of Clement is genuine." Cf. his *Early Egyptian Christianity*, 21. For a summary account of finding the "Secret Gospel" and of the scholarly discussion it generated, see John Dart, *Decoding Mark* (Harrisburg, PA: Trinity Press International, 2003), 1–16.
44. M. Smith, *Clement of Alexandria and a Secret Gospel of Mark* (Cambridge, MA: Harvard University Press, 1973).

Smith found the letter withdrew it from public scholarly scrutiny. Various persons have studied the photographic evidence and made judgments either for or against its authenticity, on the basis of known Clementine style and word usage. In the absence of other corroboration of the fragment's actual existence, scholars have never resolved the possibility of it being a clever piece of forgery, either in the seventeenth or eighteenth centuries, or even by Smith himself (as some have alleged).

Acknowledging, therefore, the quite tentative value of this text, let us review its content for what it says about Mark's Gospel. It begins with information that what follows is "from the letters of the most holy Clement, the author of the *Strōmateis* (*Stromata*). To Theodore." And it proceeds immediately to an approval of Theodore's "silencing the unspeakable teachings of the Carpocratians." After several pejorative comments about them and their teachings in general terms, the letter turns to "the things they keep saying about the divinely inspired Gospel according to Mark." This is the point where the fragment becomes interesting to us. The letter asserts that

> during Peter's stay in Rome *he wrote an account of the Lord's doings,* not, however, declaring all of them, nor yet hinting at the secret ones, but selecting what he thought most useful for increasing the faith of *those who were being instructed.*
>
> But when Peter died a martyr, *Mark came over to Alexandria,* bringing both his own notes and those of Peter, from which *he transferred to his former book* the things suitable to whatever makes for progress toward knowledge. Thus he *composed a more spiritual Gospel* for the use of *those who were being perfected.*
>
> Nevertheless, he did not divulge the things not to be uttered, nor did he write down the hierophantic teaching of the Lord, but to the stories already written he added yet others and, moreover, brought in certain sayings of which he knew the interpretation would, as a mystagogue, lead the hearers into the innermost sanctuary of *that truth hidden by seven veils.*[45]

Clement thus describes both a history of the "composition" of Mark and also a progression through spiritual development in identifiable stages. The first stage consists of *those who have faith and are being*

---

45. Morton Smith, *Clement of Alexandria and a Secret Gospel of Mark* (Cambridge, MA: Harvard University Press, 1973), 446. Emphasis added.

"*instructed.*" The second stage includes *those who are progressing in knowledge and are being "perfected,"* leading ultimately to their being "hearers" in the innermost sanctuary "of that truth *hidden* by seven veils."[46]

For each of Clement's two stages, there is identified a Markan literary composition that is appropriate to the stage and *not* the present text of Mark. Thus, for "those who are being instructed" there was "the account of the Lord's doings" (τὰς πράξεις τοῦ κυρίου), a phrase not unlike Papias's τὰ ὑπὸ τοῦ κυρίου...πραχθέντα. In my view, this would be the narrative version of Q described in chapter 2 (below), perhaps in a simpler form. Then, for those who are progressing and being perfected, Clement refers to new material added to the earlier account ("he transferred to his former book"); this included some of Mark's own material, but conspicuously included material from Peter, which led to "a more spiritual Gospel." There is nothing here specifically identifying the content of these "notes" (μνήματα), but an account of Jesus' death as one obedient to God's will together with the negative portrayals of discipleship represented by Judas's betrayal and Peter's denials would be appropriate instruction for those who are "being perfected." The consequence of joining the first account with the second account does result in "a more spiritual Gospel." Indeed, that *is* the result of the analysis I pursue here, which suggests that two originally independent accounts, one of them being of Jesus' passion and death, were joined; the power and authority of the Spirit-led Son of God is thus properly understood and deepened in mystery *only* when linked to the reality of the death of Jesus the Christ: the "First" became "Last" in a way humanly unexpected; to gain one's self, one must lose one's self (Mark 8:35). Only now is it appropriate to call Mark's composition a "Gospel," as Clement recognized.

Clement writes, "Nevertheless, he yet did not divulge the things not to be uttered, nor did he write down the hierophantic teaching of the Lord, but to the stories already written he added yet others and, moreover, brought in certain sayings of which he knew the interpretation would, as a mystagogue, lead the hearers into the innermost sanctuary of that truth hidden by seven veils." Here he is only describing further the process of joining the narrative version of Q with the passion account. His phrasing

---

46. When Paul describes his mission in Corinth (1 Cor 2:6–3:1), he also describes a progression in spiritual development in two stages, leading as in Clement to a "hidden wisdom" (2:7) for the "mature."

"He yet did not divulge the things not to be uttered, nor did he write down the hierophantic teaching of the Lord" is a parallelism referring to Mark *not* including the Q discourse material itself. And the remaining phrasing refers precisely to modifications made necessary by the joining of the two accounts.

Clement thus testifies to that penultimate stage of Mark's composition history. *That* version of Mark remained in Alexandria and apparently included materials now lost to us.[47] It was a "secret" Gospel because it disclosed the "secret" of God's plan for Jesus and for all of humankind: the complete giving of self.[48]

The Venetian Tradition

There is one further item that we should not overlook, although it speaks more to the matter of connecting Mark with Egypt than with the composition history of Mark's Gospel. There is a strong tradition that the body of Mark was brought from Egypt to Venice in 828. "That a body thought to be that of St. Mark was brought to Venice at this time is generally believed to be a historical fact."[49] The circumstances under which that body was selected, taken, and transported to Venice may not be entirely clear,[50] but the respective political situations of Alexandria and Venice in the ninth century make the tradition plausible. Alexandria was in decline under Arab rule after Cairo was made the new capital, and Christian shrines would have experienced a sense of vulnerability. Venice, on the other hand, was in its ascendancy under Doge Giustiniano Participazio and in need of a strong religious symbol and patron to assure its independence of the Western Empire. Bringing a body to Venice and identifying it as "St. Mark" would accomplish nothing if there were no strong tradition, *commonly known and accepted,* that St. Mark had actually been buried in Alexandria, Egypt.

---

47. Thus, the excerpt mentioned by Clement is this letter fragment of material between Mark 10:34 and Mark 10:35, material that blends elements of the blind Bartimaeus story with the Johannine raising of Lazarus.
48. John Dominic Crossan thus comments concerning the *Gospel of Thomas:* "The Gospel of Thomas begins by announcing that it contains *secret* sayings from Jesus. Since these utterances have been written down for anyone to read, however, their secrecy is not a matter of physical concealment but of concealed meaning." J. D. Crossan, "Paradise Regained: A Commentary," in *Unearthing the Lost Words of Jesus: The Discovery and Text of the Gospel of Thomas* (ed. J. Dart and R. Riegert; Berkeley, CA: Seastone, 1998), 95.
49. John Julius Norwich, *A History of Venice* (New York: Knopf, 1982), 29.
50. For a summary of the accounts, see ibid., 28–30.

I mention the "Venetian Connection" here as a tradition since it lends some additional weight to the affirmations, reported above and continued even today by the Coptic Church, that Mark went to Egypt and was buried there.

The (Patristic) History of the Composition of Mark

I mentioned at the beginning that the testimonies of the early church writers were, on the surface, confusing if all were to be understood as referring to our present text of Mark, composed as a single entity. They variously affirm that "Mark" was written both in Egypt and in Rome, independently of Peter and dependent upon Peter's teaching, with the disinterested knowledge of Peter and with his authoritative approval. My proposal of stages of composition based on the narrative characteristics of Mark, however, removes that confusion and, in turn, seems to be supported by the patristic witness itself.

Papias states that Mark wrote "the things said and done by the Lord" and "not as an arrangement/ordered account of the Lord's sayings." I suggest that this remembers Mark's narrative version of Q (chap. 2, below). Clement's comment in the letter to Theodore ("he wrote an account of the Lord's doings") seems to refer also to this.

Both Clement and Papias agree on Mark's writing *after* he became associated with Peter, but Clement adds the information that Mark had followed Peter "a long time" before being with him in Rome.

Clement states that it was in Rome that Peter preached "the gospel," and Mark was urged by "many" to write it down, "nor did they cease until they had prevailed." Since "the gospel" concerned "the Christ," and Paul provides a parallel understanding of "the gospel," I propose that these testimonies refer to the Passion Account (chap. 3, below). When Peter learned what Mark was doing, he neither encouraged nor discouraged it (Clement).

Peter left Rome, and so too did Mark (Clement), going to Egypt (Eusebius; Jerome; Clement, to Theodore), where he preached "the gospel [the Passion Account] which he had also put into writing" (Eusebius). At this point, it seems, the narrative version of Q and the Passion Narrative were not yet joined.

In Egypt, Mark was the first to establish churches in Alexandria (Eusebius), which attracted the admiration of Philo (Jerome). The departure of

Peter from Rome *may* have been occasioned by Claudius's expulsion of all Jews (c. 49), and the conjunction of "Mark" and "Philo" in Jerome's testimony also suggests a time frame in the late 40s. Clement remembers that during this period Mark joined the Passion Narrative to the narrative version of Q (letter to Theodore), resulting in "a more spiritual Gospel" (chap. 4, below).

Mark dies in Egypt in 62 (Eusebius) and was buried in Alexandria (Jerome).

Thus by 62 CE at least a text largely comparable to our present text of Mark existed. One version of it remained in Alexandria (Clement, to Theodore), with some materials at variance with our present text. Because one could understand its meaning, its "truth hidden by seven veils," only when by reading it as a whole, it was a "secret" Gospel, "for the use of those who were being perfected" (Clement, to Theodore). Whether some or all of the narratives exemplifying discipleship were added before 62 is not clear from the patristic witness.

At some point the "Gospel" is authorized by Peter to be read in all the churches (independent tradition, attached to Clement's testimony by Eusebius). One can only speculate that Peter did so to honor Mark, who "had followed him for a long time."

The tradition associating Mark with Rome may well coincide with this approval. Certainly the references to *persecution* in the emendations made to the eschatological discourse in chapter 13 could later be understood in light of the upheavals in Rome around 70 CE (see chap. 4, below). When John Donahue reviewed the divergent opinions on the "enduring question"[51] of when, where, and for whom the Gospel of Mark was written, he concluded that "there is no consensus on the setting of Mark, nor is there a method agreed upon for describing the social makeup of a given community on the basis of a text."[52] Donahue argues that Mark was "written" for a Roman community around 70, largely because of the materials I will identify[53] as later emendations to an earlier narrative. So, too, would the discipleship passages — which emphasize the complete giving of all one has, even one's life (6:14–29; 12:41–44; 14:3–9) — be consistent with that later set of circumstances. And the

---

51. J. R. Donahue, "Windows and Mirrors: The Setting of Mark's Gospel," *Catholic Biblical Quarterly* 57, no. 1 (January 1995): 1.
52. Ibid., 2.
53. See chap. 4, section on "The Community."

review of the whole text by one or more individuals, adding explanatory phrasings, would be consistent with a community of Christians thoroughly unfamiliar with Jewish customs and Aramaic phrasings.[54] Perhaps precisely these revisions to the "more spiritual Gospel" from Alexandria made it a text that could be used "wherever the good news is preached" (Mark 14:9).

---

54. See chap. 5, section on "Explanatory Glosses."

Chapter Two

A Narrative Version of "Q"

Introduction

About Q and Its Content

Before stating the relationship of Mark to "Q," it is best for me to clarify what I understand by Q. What biblical scholars speak of as Q is, admittedly, dependent upon a hypothesis. As an effort to explain the relationships among the Gospels of Matthew, Mark, and Luke, they asserted that Matthew and Luke employed the Gospel of Mark as a source for much of their narrative materials and for the basic sequence of events in Jesus' life.[1] Once they accepted the arguments for Mark's priority as persuasive, it was also necessary to resort to another "source" (*Quelle*, in German), identified as Q, to account for the degree of similarity in Matthew's and Luke's reporting of the sayings of Jesus.[2] This so-called Two Document Hypothesis has been the bedrock of much scholarly work in the latter part of the twentieth century.[3] Indeed, "in the last twenty years the pursuit of Q has become a considerable industry."[4] Some have challenged the Q hypothesis, however, particularly in the last decade,[5] and

---

1. B. H. Streeter gave the classic expression of the arguments for the priority of Mark, in *The Four Gospels* (London: Macmillan, 1924), 159ff.
2. For a recent review of "the major turning points in the history of Q research," cf. James M. Robinson, "Introduction," in *The Sayings Gospel Q in Greek and English: With Parallels from the Gospels of Mark and Thomas* (ed. J. M. Robinson, P. Hoffmann, and J. Kloppenborg; Minneapolis: Fortress, 2002), 11–72.
3. The redaction-criticism analyses of the Gospels of Matthew and Luke, detailing the manner in which each altered Mark's text and suggesting what can be learned from that, is "directly dependent on [this] particular solution to the Synoptic problem.... The reopening of the Synoptic problem in recent debates has thus been potentially to call into question the value of a large number of redaction-critical studies of the Gospels," as stated by C. Tuckett, *Reading the New Testament: Methods of Interpretation* (Philadelphia: Fortress, 1987), 119.
4. M. D. Goulder, "Is Q a Juggernaut?" *Journal of Biblical Literature* 115, no. 4 (1996): 667.
5. In the last decade Michael Goulder (ibid., 667–81) and Mark S. Goodacre (*The Synoptic Problem: A Way through the Maze* [Biblical Seminar; London: Sheffield Academic Press, 2001]

in appendix 1 I offer a test case and other considerations that make the latest challenges (catchingly called the "Mark without Q Hypothesis") to the Q hypothesis more problematic than what they seek to replace.[6]

What I understand about "Q" here is this: When Matthew and Luke agree substantially on the wording of sayings that their Gospels attribute to Jesus, those two evangelists have taken them from a stratum of early Christian traditions. We should not understand this stratum to have been a document (no copy of "Q" has ever been found[7]), but should think of it as a stable complex of Jesus' sayings and widely known among the early Christian churches. The reconstruction of the content of Q is, in turn, dependent upon other judgments concerning whether one should follow the sequence of the sayings in Luke or in Matthew and whether the wording of one evangelist should be consistently preferred to the other's. Here I assume the arguments John Kloppenborg has made in favor of Luke's sequence for the Q sayings material.[8]

As a widely known and respected stratum of the sayings of Jesus, Q would have been representative of the interpretation of Jesus in the primitive Christian community. That is not to say that it did not present side-by-side interpretations that from our vantage point seem to be in tension. Accepting the traditional reconstructions of Q, there are clearly materials that interpret Jesus in the context of Jewish wisdom speculation and others that sharply articulate an apocalyptic view.[9] These are not entirely mutually exclusive; when the Jewish wisdom tradition speaks of the two "ways," one of which leads to life and the other to death, it has prepared for a saying such as Mark 8:38, "For whoever is ashamed of

---

and *The Case against Q: Studies in Markan Priority and the Synoptic Problem* [Harrisburg, PA: Trinity Press International, 2002]) have both argued that the Synoptic relationships can be best resolved by Matthew's enlarging Mark's Gospel and Luke's subsequent use of both of those Gospels.

6. Christopher Tuckett provides the sane caution: "We shall never be able to 'prove' that one solution to the Synoptic problem is right with the degree of finality which we could achieve in a mathematical proof. The nature of the evidence simply will not allow it" (*Reading the New Testament: Methods of Interpretation* [Philadelphia: Fortress, 1987], 80).

7. To speak of a "critical edition" is, accordingly, an unfortunate choice of words for what is an impressive sifting of scholarly opinion about the recurrence of some of the sayings attributed to Jesus across the writings of early Christianity. See J. M. Robinson, P. Hoffmann, and J. S. Kloppenborg, eds., *The Critical Edition of Q: Synopsis Including the Gospels of Matthew and Luke, Mark and Thomas* (Louvain: Peeters, 2000).

8. Cf. J. S. Kloppenborg, *Q Parallels: Synopsis, Critical Notes, and Concordance* (Foundations and Facets, NT; Sonoma, CA: Polebridge, 1988), xxiii–xxx.

9. John S. Kloppenborg has used these differences to suggest a history of sorts for the Q materials, in *The Formation of Q: Trajectories in Ancient Wisdom Collections* (Studies in Antiquity and Christianity; Philadelphia: Fortress, 1987; Harrisburg, PA: Trinity Press International, 1999).

me and of my words in this adulterous and sinful generation, the Son of Man will also be ashamed of him when he comes in the glory of his Father with the holy angels"[10] On the one hand, the words of Jesus are seen to give the critically good "way" to live wisely before God, and on the other hand, the consequence of failing to attend to that teaching is a "way" that will be judged by the apocalyptic Son of Man. In the Q materials the blending of these two themes, the sapiential and the apocalyptic, may well be representative of the range of early Christian thought and not indications of stages of the history of early Christianity.

When I speak (below) of the relationship of Mark to Q and of his occasionally employing, it seems, some of Q's language, I do not mean that in such cases Mark has made a conscious transfer of Q materials into narrative, but rather that Mark has given a narrative form or representation to the interpretation of Jesus that Q represents. We are not, therefore, to think of Q as a documentary "source" or text employed by Mark. Instead, we can think of Q as the "occasion"[11] behind what I call Mark's narrative version of Q (QN).

About Mark and Q

To review the history of biblical scholarship on the relationship between Mark and Q is not necessary here. In 1993 Christopher M. Tuckett wrote a *status quaestionis* that reviewed the discussion to that point[12]; since then the work of Harry Fleddermann[13] has prompted a renewed interest in the question of whether "Mark" (the text) was literarily dependent upon "Q" (in its final, textual form), including a considered evaluation by Frans Neirynck in 1996.[14] But almost a decade after Tuckett's survey,

---

10. Scripture translations are my own unless otherwise identified. For an assessment and reaffirmation of the presence of "Son of Man" in Mark 8:38, cf. J. Lambrecht, "A Note on Mark 8.38 and Q 12.8–9," *Journal for the Study of the New Testament* 85 (2002): 117–25.

11. As a parallel example consider the way in which the popular hymn "Amazing Grace" was occasioned by New Testament texts and presents those texts in a different, more poignant form.

12. C. Tuckett, "Mark and Q," in *The Synoptic Gospels: Source Criticism and the New Literary Criticism* (ed. Camille Focant; Bibliotheca ephemeridum theologicarum lovaniensium 110; Louvain: Leuven University Press / Peeters, 1993), 149–75. An earlier appraisal was made by D. Lührmann, "The Gospel of Mark and the Sayings Collection Q," *Journal of Biblical Literature* 108, no. 1 (1989): 51–71.

13. H. T. Fleddermann, *Mark and Q: A Study of the Overlap Texts* (Bibliotheca ephemeridum theologicarum lovaniensium 122; Louvain: Leuven University Press / Peeters, 1995). Cf. the review article by J. Verheyden, "Mark and Q," *Ephemerides theologicae lovanienses* 72, no. 4 (1996): 408–17.

14. F. Neirynck, "The Sayings Source Q and the Gospel of Mark," in *Geschichte — Tradition — Reflexion: Festschrift für Martin Hengel zum 70. Geburtstag* (ed. H. Cancik, H. Lichtenberger, and P. Schäfer; Tübingen: Mohr [Siebeck], 1996), 125–45.

it was the judgment of Andreas Schmidt in 2001 that "the question of whether or not there is a direct relationship between the Gospel of Mark and Q, the Sayings Source, is still wide open."[15] As recognized above, the focus here is not on a direct, literary dependence of Mark upon a text of Q, but rather Mark's elaboration of the themes and theology presented in Q in Mark's own, narrative form.[16] Let us turn to that now.

Leaving aside for now the verb-less phrasing in Mark 1:1, which stands as a title for the entire Gospel,[17] the first story the reader/hearer encounters immediately introduces a strong narrative line: God, in keeping with his long-known plan (1:2–3, 4–7), has broken into human history (v. 10) to identify Jesus of Nazareth (v. 9) as the one who would, as his "beloved Son" (v. 11), be the bearer of God's Spirit (v. 10) and announce that "The present age has reached its end and the kingdom of God has come near" (v. 15). Everything that follows in this story line focuses on Jesus, the breaking apart of the control over the present age by Jesus' actions against the demonic, and Jesus' teaching on the kingdom of God, entered by doing the will of God, with judgment by the future Son of Man. The redactor has at points overlaid this story line with perspectives reflecting the other story lines present in Mark's Gospel, distinguishable because of their particular features. Nevertheless, its features are clear: a *focus on Jesus* (unaccompanied by disciples, usually) in an *eschatological context, the central importance of the kingdom of God, an emphasis on personally doing the will of God* (as opposed, e.g., to discipleship to Jesus) because one has *"faith,"* meaning a recognition of the authority present in Jesus, and the *future judgment of the Son of Man*. A reconstruction of this material appears in a later section of this chapter.

Broadly speaking, this first distinctive story line appears concentrated in Mark 1:2 to 13:32. Some passages within this block of material appear to stand in tension with the prominent features of the story narrated there, and I will discuss them below. But first let us focus upon the phenomenon of the parallels between Mark and Q, all of which fall within

---

15. M. Labahn and A. Schmidt, eds., *Jesus, Mark, and Q: The Teaching of Jesus and Its Earliest Records* (JSNTSupp 214; Sheffield: Sheffield Academic Press, 2001), 14.

16. Cf. Burton L. Mack for the view that "Q represents a written tradition," that "Mark 'knew' Q in some or several versions, while choosing not to incorporate all of its material," and that this is a matter of Mark's manner of treating an earlier "text": in "Q and the Gospel of Mark; Revising Christian Origins," *Semeia* 55 (1991): 22, 25.

17. Thus, e.g., E. LaVerdiere, *The Beginning of the Gospel: Introducing the Gospel according to Mark*, vol. 1, *Mark 1–8:21* (Collegeville, MN: Liturgical Press, 1999), 1–4.

this block of materials and the distinctive story line shown in detail below. Both the textual parallels and the narrative similarities lead us to call this stage of Mark's composition a "narrative version of Q," that early collection of the sayings of Jesus reconstructed by scholarly argument.[18]

The Textual Parallels between Mark and Q

At a number of places in Mark's text, both the wording and the context suggest a parallel between Mark's Gospel and the collection of Jesus' sayings in Q (generally following Luke's versification below).[19]

Mark		
1:2–3	=	Q 3:2–4
1:7–8	=	Q 3:16b–17
1:9–11	=	Q 3:21–22
1:12–13	=	Q 4:1
3:22–29	=	Q 11:15–18; 12:10
4:24–25	=	Q 6:38; 19:26
4:30–32	=	Q 13:18–19
6:8–12	=	Q 10:4–11
8:11–12	=	Q 11:16, 29
8:34–35	=	Q 14:27; 17:33
8:38	=	Luke 9:26–27
9:37	=	Luke 9:48
9:42	=	Q 17:1–2
9:50	=	Luke 14:34
10:31	=	Q 13:30
12:38b–39	=	Q 11:43
13:11	=	Q 12:11

It is immediately apparent that the sequence of these parallels is not the same in the two traditions (nor in Matthew either). The verbal contacts are strong enough to assert that the Markan tradition knew the sayings also reported by Q, but the difference in sequence suggests two

---

18. The most recent presentation of the content of "Q" has been advanced in a "critical edition" (!) of this hypothetical source: Robinson et al., *Critical Edition of Q*.
19. The texts mentioned here largely follow Kloppenborg's observations in his *Q Parallels*, passim, but I have omitted the parallels that Kloppenborg finds at Mark 1:21 (Q 7:1); 4:21 (Q 11:33). Added to Kloppenborg's assessment are Mark 8:38; 9:37; and 9:50, following the judgment of Fleddermann, *Mark and Q*, passim. We are following Kloppenborg's convention of identifying Q passages according to the Lukan chapter and verse designations, except for the three texts from Fleddermann's study.

possibilities: Mark's tradition may have known the sayings tradition *before* it acquired the stable, fixed form now labeled as Q; or the framer of Mark's tradition may have freely selected from among those materials.

What is of significant interest, however, is that *all* of these parallels appear within the block Mark 1:2–13:32, which appears to be a narrative version of the Q material, with a replication of Q's emphases in Mark's story line.[20]

The Narrative Parallels between Mark and Q

Far more striking, however, is the paralleling of the story line presented in this block of Markan material and Q. The difference between a (somewhat coherent) collection of the sayings of Jesus (Q)[21] and a narrative account of Jesus' deeds (Mark's narrative version of Q) is certainly enormous. Yet a comparison of the two finds a number of points of agreement. *Both* thus

- begin with John's preaching about the Coming One and a reference to the "Holy Spirit" (Q 3:16b–17 // Mark 1:7–8),
- refer to Jesus' temptations in the wilderness (Q 4:1–13 // Mark 1:12–13),
- have Jesus proclaiming the kingdom of God (Q 16:16; 10:9; 11:20 // Mark 1:14–15),
- have Jesus speak of the kingdom of God in parables (Q 13:18–20 // Mark 4:26–32),
- attribute authority to Jesus (Q 7:(1–7) 8 // Mark 1:27; 11:28–33),
- refer to the [future!] Son of Man as guarantor of Jesus and of response to Jesus (Q 12:8–9 // Mark 8:38),
- have Jesus' reaction to a lack of faith in Israel (Q 7:1–10 // Mark 6:2–6),

---

20. *The Critical Edition of Q*, by Robinson et al., indicates a number of *additional* parallels within this block of material. *All* but the parallels to Mark 11:9b–10, 22, and five parallels to Mark 13 occur in the reconstructed text of Mark's narrative version of Q in a following section of this chapter.

21. Even as reconstructed, Q is a mix of narrative and discourse, alternated, and the discourse materials are topically organized. Perhaps the genre of the "Sayings of the Wise" has been too determinative in assessing Q to date, since in addition to the baptism and temptation accounts, there is at least one other narrative piece in Q; perhaps others have been omitted from the reconstructions of Q precisely because they appeared to be narrative. That alternation of narrative and discourse is the pattern in the Gospel of Matthew, and the pattern of narrative and "interlude" characterizes the Gospel of Mark: H. M. Humphrey, *"He Is Risen!" A New Reading of Mark's Gospel* (New York: Paulist Press, 1992).

- have Jesus asking about the role of the Baptist (Q 7:24–28 // Mark 11:29–30),

- portray Jesus' affirming of the law (Q16:16–17 // Mark 10:18–19),

- have Jesus' words for mission (Q 10:4–11 // Mark 6:8–11),

- refer to the disciples as "salt" (Q14:34–35 // Mark 9:50),

- have opponents align Jesus with the devil (Q11:15 // Mark 3:22) and give Jesus' response (Q 11:17–18 // Mark 3:23–25),

- speak of the (ultimate, final, eschatological) reversal of first and last (Q 13:30 // Mark 10:31), and

- have Jesus' eschatological discourse at the end (Q 17:23–24, 26–30, 34–35, 37 // Mark 13:5–32, passim) and include a reference to the Son of Man at the end (Q 17:30 // Mark 13:26–27).

In view of these many parallels of emphasis, the differences between a discourse collection (Q) and Mark's narrative account diminish. They run as parallel presentations, both in their scope and in their portrayals of Jesus. As to the scope of the presentation, both open with the proclamation of the eschatological inbreaking of the kingdom of God, and both end with an eschatological discourse, warning about being ready for the coming of the Son of Man. As to their portrayals of Jesus, both show Jesus to be graced with the Spirit of God at his baptism and led by the Spirit and aware that opposition to himself is opposition to the Spirit present in him (Q 12:10 // Mark 3:29). Mark, consequently, portrays Jesus as speaking and acting with authority, an authority that he confers upon disciples in the last days of the present generation, before the coming of the Son of Man in judgment. Significantly, these references to the Son of Man are never to a figure who will suffer and die, but to a future guarantor of Jesus' words and deeds.

Because of these parallels of scope of presentation and portrayal of Jesus, it is appropriate to speak of the consistent narrative identified in Mark 1:2–13:32 (passim) and shown in a later section as "a narrative version of Q," here called "QN." (Even a cursory scanning of QN shows that most of the discourse materials that Mark attributes to Jesus and are not also "overlaps" with Q occur within this block of material; in that respect also, QN strikingly parallels Q's characteristic feature.)

A Distinctive Narrative Feature of Mark's Version of Q: Jesus Is the "Holy Son of God"

The narrative makes it explicitly clear that Jesus is God's "Son" (1:11) upon whom God's "Spirit" has descended (1:10) and who is acknowledged as the "Holy One of God" by the unclean spirits (1:24). I have suggested elsewhere[22] that one way to read the present text of Mark is to notice the emphasis at the beginning on Jesus as the "Son of God" graced with the presence of the "Spirit" of God, and to view this against the background provided by the Wisdom of Solomon. A parallel between the two presentations appears much more specifically when one views only Mark 1:2–13:32.

The Wisdom of Solomon introduces us to the "righteous man" who calls God "father" and so is God's "son." We read of the righteous king, the author of the text and so, one surmises, the "Solomon" of the title. In giving a strong description of the "Wisdom of God," the text of Wisdom of Solomon becomes pertinent to my purposes here. When one lists all the things that "Wisdom" does in the Wisdom of Solomon, that list parallels what the book also describes the "righteous man" and the "righteous king" as doing.

The text says that Wisdom

- has knowledge of God (Wis 8:4; 9:9–11, 17–18),
- has knowledge of the law (Wis 6:17–18; 9:9 [cf. Sir 24]),
- appeals to men to learn wisdom (Wis 6:13, 16 [cf. Prov 1:20–21; 8:15; 9:3–6]),
- upbraids/warns men about "sins" ([cf. Prov 1:23–31]),
- offers blessing/good things (Wis 7:11; 8:5; 9:18c [cf. Prov 3:13–18; 8:21, 35]),
- offers intimacy with Wisdom's self (Wis 6:12–13, 16; 8:9, 16 [cf. Prov 1:33; 4:6, 13; 7:4; 8:17])
- and with God (Wis 7:14, 27–28).

But that portrayal is mirrored in the presentations of the two paradigmatic figures in the Wisdom of Solomon, the righteous man and Solomon himself, who become illustrations of the principle expressed in Wis 7:27:

---

22. Ibid.

A Narrative Version of "Q"

"In every generation she [Wisdom] passes into holy souls and makes them friends of God, and prophets" (NRSV)

The text also says that the righteous man and the Righteous King have

- knowledge of God (Wis 2:13; 7:15–22),
- knowledge of the law (2:12; 6:17–20),
- appeals to men (6:1–11, 21–25),
- warns men about sins (2:12, 16; 6:4–8),
- offers blessings (2:16; 6:10, 19–20),
- offers intimacy with Solomon's self (7:13)
- and with God (2:16; 7:14).

The key to these presentations appears in the text of Wis 7:27. Thus the "righteous man" and the "righteous king" do what Wisdom does *precisely because* Wisdom has entered into them. Wisdom loves those who love her and abides with them (6:12, 16; 8:16). And Wisdom is spirit (7:22).

These activities of Wisdom, the righteous man, and the righteous king find a further parallel in the activities of what Jesus does in Mark 1:2–13:32 (the texts in *italics* are from Mark's version of Q, as identified below):

- Knowledge of what God requires (Mark *7:14–23; 10:6–9, 17–52*).
- Knowledge of God's plan (*1:14;* 4:11; 8:31, *34; 13:20, 27*).
- Appeals to hearers to respond to his teaching (*1:14, 38; 4:9*).
- Warns about sins (*7:8–13; 12:14–17, 18–27*)
- and particularly about sins against the law.
- Like the righteous man, opposes actions of ungodly (*8:15; 11:27–28; 12:1–12, 38–40*).
- Offers blessings [does miracles], promises and blessings in kingdom of God, and eternal life (4:20; *10:29–30*).
- Offers intimacy with Jesus' self (*1:22; 3:13–14, 34–35; 6:31; etc.*)
- and with God (*10:14–15*).

The Distinctive Vocabulary of QN

A distinctive vocabulary would, not unexpectedly, accompany a distinctive story line. Since I am advancing the distinctive story line identified here as a thesis, however, it is quite significant to find a distinctive vocabulary virtually restricted to this reconstruction. The internal evidence of the text shows this vocabulary as prominently featured in this "narrative version of Q," and absent or almost absent from the other Markan materials.

The vocabulary recognized here includes the following terms:

- *Kingdom of God* appears 14 times in Mark, 11 of which are in QN.[23]

- *Son of Man* appears 14 times in Mark, and two of the three clear instances of the phrase as a reference to a *future* figure are in QN (8:38 and 13:26).[24]

- *Authority/Power* (ἐξουσία) appears 10 times in Mark, with *all* except 13:34 in QN.

- *Teaching* (διδαχή) appears 5 times in Mark, with *all* except 11:18 in QN.

- *Teach* (διδάσκω) appears 17 times in Mark, with *all* except 2:13; 12:35; 14:49 in QN.

- *Teacher* (διδάσκαλος) appears 12 times in Mark, with *all* except 10:35; 14:14 in QN.[25] (Taken together, the "teach-" cognates appear 34 times in Mark, with only 6 usages outside QN.)

- *Spirit* (πνεῦμα) appears 23 times in Mark, with *all* except 12:36; 13:11; 14:38 in QN.

- *Generation* (γενεά) appears only 5 times in Mark, and *all* are in QN.

- *Understand* (συνίημι) appears only 5 times in Mark, with *all* except 4:12 in QN.

---

23. In the overall block of material, Mark 1:2–13:32, only 4:11 has been seen as not belonging to QN; the other two usages of kingdom of God appear at 14:25 and 15:43.

24. The third reference occurs in Mark 14:62c, a phrasing added when QN and PN were assimilated; see chapter three. There are also two instances of Son of Man that are ambiguous, Mark 2:10 and 2:28, where the reference could be either to a future figure or to a present Jesus. Both of these are in QN. All the remaining instances of Son of Man are clearly a reference to the suffering Son of Man: Mark 8:31; 9:9; 9:12; 9:31; 10:33; 10:45; 14:21 (2x); 14:41; and 14:62a, b.

25. Mark 14:14 not only stands outside the block 1:2–13:32, but also differs from most other instances of "Teacher" in that it is not used in direct address but as a title.

- *House* (οἰκία) appears 18 times in Mark, with *all* except 2:15; 13:35; 14:3 in QN.

- *Privately* (κατ' ἰδίαν) appears 7 times in Mark, with *all* in QN except 4:34.

Taken as a matrix of sorts, these eleven terms appear 100 out of 132 times in QN, or 76 percent. Their frequent repetition in this narrative shapes the way we hear and understand the narrative. Moreover, the relative absence of these terms outside the QN material serves to identify a different narrative world, in which other terms and interpretations determine the hearer/reader's response.

Summary of the Characteristic Features of QN in Mark

Overall, the material identified here as a narrative version of Q, like Q itself, focuses on the importance of Jesus' teaching for eternal life. The eschatological kingdom of God is breaking in, and response to Jesus' teaching will be subject to the judgment of the Son of Man in the near future. The Christology is, accordingly, "low": Jesus is the one commissioned by God and led by God's Spirit. Though QN speaks of Jesus as the "Holy One of God" and the "Son of God," these terms are used in the sense of the "Righteous One" of Wisdom, chapters 2 and 7. There is not even a trace here of a messianic Christology; there are no references to "Christ" or "kingdom of David" or "King of the Jews," motifs that appear in other composition layers of Mark's Gospel, particularly in the Passion Narrative material reviewed in chapter 3 (below).

Because the focus is upon the immediate response to Jesus' teaching and the nearness of the judgment by the Son of Man, there is, not surprisingly, no ecclesiology of any kind. Nor is there an interest in "discipleship," as opposed to "disciples." Jesus indeed calls disciples, but calls them in order to extend his own work in view of the impending, near kingdom of God. There is certainly no sense of the disciples as "models" of true discipleship for subsequent generations; indeed, there is no concern for subsequent generations at all (see Mark 10:29–30).

Preliminary Suggestions about the Provenance of QN

At this point, only two suggestions appear to be supported by the observations made above.

1. The parallels between QN and the Wisdom of Solomon could not exist without the latter work having been influential upon the author/compiler of QN. That in turn means that he/she had access to the Septuagint. Since there is no evidence to date that the Septuagint circulated within Palestine proper, that suggests an author whose Jewish experience and library were to be found in Diaspora Judaism. In trying to narrow the reference to the Diaspora, the association of the Wisdom of Solomon with Alexandria, coupled with the strong tradition associating Mark with Egyptian Christianity reported in chapter 1 (above), is intriguing.

2. In view of the "low Christology" represented by the materials in QN and in view of the insistence that the judgment by the Son of Man is in the near future, a relatively early dating for this compilation of materials seems a logical position, as it does for Q itself. Anticipating materials I later present and arguments I later make, "early" may be taken as late 30s or early 40s of the first century. Certainly the absence of a developed messianic Christology, as represented by the use of "Christ" as a familiar title (without the article) as early as Paul's letters in the early 50s, suggests a period before the 50s. So, too, does the absence of a clear ecclesiology, which is emerging in Paul's letters and later developed in Matthew, for example.

Mark's Narrative Version of Q

1:2 *Just as it is written in Isaiah the prophet,*[26]
"**Behold I send my messenger before your face,
who will prepare your way:**

1:3 **a voice crying out in the desert,
'Make ready the way of the Lord,
Make his paths straight.'** "

1:4 *There was John,*
baptizing in the desert

---

26. The translation used here is my own. The text of Mark has been arranged in such a way as to highlight the transitional seams (indicated by text in italics) between materials and to distinguish narrative material from sayings material. Also italicized are phrasings explaining Aramaic terms or Jewish traditions found in the traditional materials; no judgment is intended on whether these were made at the same time as this narrative version of Q. The phrasings in Mark's text that are alleged to reflect the specific wording of Q material are indicated by bold print.

A Narrative Version of "Q"

	and preaching a baptism of repentance for the forgiveness of sins.
1:5	And all the country of Judea went out to him, and all the people of Jerusalem, and they were baptized by him in the river Jordan, confessing their sins.
1:6	And John was clothed with the hair of a camel and with a leather girdle about his waist, and he was eating locusts and wild honey.
1:7	*And he proclaimed publicly,* **"One is coming after me who is more powerful than I, before whom I am not worthy** even to bend down and **untie the thong of his sandals.**
1:8	*I* have baptized you with water, but *he* will baptize you with a holy spirit."
1:9	*And it happened at that time that* Jesus from Nazareth of Galilee went and was baptized in the Jordan by John.
1:10	*And immediately as he was coming up out of the water, he saw the heavens being split apart and the Spirit coming down upon him like a dove;*
1:11	*and a voice came out of the heavens,* "You are my beloved Son; with you I am well pleased."
1:12	*And immediately the Spirit drove him out into the wilderness.*
1:13	And he was in the wilderness forty days while being tested by Satan, and he was among the monstrous, and the angels took care of him.
1:14	*But after John was handed over Jesus came into Galilee, preaching the "good news" of God*
1:15	and saying: "The present age has reached its end and the kingdom of God has come near; Repent! And believe in the 'good news'!"
1:16	*And passing along by the Sea of Galilee,*

	he saw Simon and Simon's brother, Andrew, casting a net into the sea (*for they were fishermen.*)
1:17	And Jesus said to them,
	"Come with me and I will make you into fishers of men!"
1:18	And immediately, leaving the nets, they followed him.
1:19	*And, having gone a short distance,*
	he saw James the son of Zebedee and John his brother as they were mending the nets in their boat,
1:20	and he immediately called out to them.
	And, leaving their father, Zebedee, in the boat with the hired workers, they followed him.
1:21	*And [they] entered into Capharnaum.*
	And immediately, going into the synagogue, he taught.
1:22	*And* they were amazed at his teaching,
	for he was teaching them like one who has authority
	and not the way the scribes taught.
1:23	*And immediately*
	there was *in their synagogue* a man with an unclean spirit,
	and he cried out
1:24	"What is there between us and you, Jesus Nazarene?
	Have you come to destroy us?
	I know who you are: THE HOLY ONE OF GOD!"
1:25	And Jesus rebuked him,
	"Be quiet! Come out of the man!"
1:26	And the unclean spirit, convulsing the man
	and crying out with a loud noise, left him.
1:27	And everyone was astounded, so that they asked one another:
	"What's this?
	A new teaching, given with authority!
	And he gives orders to the unclean spirits, and they obey him!"
1:28	*And the report of this went out everywhere into all the neighboring region of Galilee.*
1:29	*And, immediately after leaving the synagogue,*
	they went into Simon and Andrew's home, with James and John.
1:30	*But* Simon's mother-in-law was in bed, sick with a fever;
	and they immediately told him about her.

1:31	And coming over to her,
	he lifted her up while holding her hand tightly;
	and the fever left her,
	and she served them.
1:32	*When evening came and the sun had set,*
	they brought to him all those who were sick or possessed by demons;
1:33	*and the whole city was gathered in front of the door.*
1:34	*And he healed many who were sick from various diseases,*
	and he cast out many demons,
	and he would not allow the demons to speak, because they knew who he was.
1:35	*And very early in the morning while it was still dark*
	he got up and went out and went into a desolate place; and he prayed there.
1:36	*And Simon and those who were with him searched for him;*
1:37	*and they found him*
	and said to him,
	"Every one is looking for you!"
1:38	And he said to them,
	"Let us go from here to the next towns,
	so that I may preach there also;
	for it is for this that I have come out."
1:39	*And he went preaching in their synagogues and casting out demons throughout all of Galilee.*
1:40	*And* a leper came to him, appealing to him
	and saying,
	"If you want to, you are able to make me clean."
1:41	And, compassionately, he reached out his hand and touched him
	and said to him,
	"I do want to; be clean!"
1:42	And the leprosy left him immediately
	and the man was made clean.
1:43	And snorting indignantly at the man,
	he immediately sent him away and [1:44] said to him,
	"Take care that you don't say anything to anyone,
	but go and show yourself to the priest

	and present the things Moses has prescribed for your cleansing,
	as a witness to them."
1:45	But when the man went out, he began to preach everywhere and to spread the story around
	so that it was no longer possible for Jesus to go openly into a town;
	but he was out in deserted places,
	and they came to him from all directions.
2:1	*And when he again went into Capharnaum a few days later*
	"He's home!" was heard.
2:2	*And so many came together that not even the space in front of the door could any longer hold them;*
	and he proclaimed "the Word" to them.
2:3	*And they approached him,* carrying a paralytic held by four men.
2:4	And, not being able to bring the man to him because of the crowd,
	they removed the roof where he was,
	and, after making a hole, they lowered the stretcher where the paralytic lay ill.
2:5	And Jesus, seeing their faith,
	said to the paralytic,
	"My child, your sins are being forgiven."
2:6	But there were some of the scribes sitting there
	and debating among themselves privately,
2:7	"What is this man saying in effect? He blasphemes!
	Who can forgive sins except the one God?"
2:8	And Jesus, immediately realizing inside himself
	that they were debating among themselves in this way,
	said to them,
	"Why do you debate these things among yourselves?
2:9	Which is the easier thing,
	to say to the paralytic
	'Your sins are being forgiven'
	or to say
	'Get up and take your stretcher and walk?'
2:10	In order for you to know, however, that
	'The Son of Man has power to forgive sins on earth,'
	(he said to the paralytic)

2:11	I say to you, Get up! Take your stretcher and go home!"

2:12	And he got up,
	  and promptly picking up the stretcher,
	  he went away in full view of everybody,
	  so that everyone was astonished and glorifying God saying,
	    "Never have we seen the like of this!"

3:7	*And Jesus withdrew with his disciples to the sea.*
	And an enormous crowd followed:
	  from Galilee
	  and from Judea

3:8	and from Jerusalem and from Idumea and beyond the Jordan and from around Tyre and Sidon, *an enormous crowd, hearing how much he did, went to him.*

3:9	And he told his disciples that a small boat should
	  be made ready on account of the crowd,
	    lest they should crush him.

3:10	*For he had healed many*
	  so that all those with afflictions pushed towards him in order
	    to touch him.

3:11	*And the unclean spirits, whenever they saw him,*
	  would fall down before him and cry out,
	    "You are **THE SON OF GOD!"**

3:12	*and he many times rebuked them* *lest they should make him known.*
3:13	*And he went up into the hills* *and* called to himself those whom he wanted, and they went to him.
3:14	that they might be with him and that he might send them to preach
3:15	and to have authority to expel demons;

3:21	*And learning about it,*
	  those who were close to him went out to restrain him,
	  for they said,
	    "He's out of his mind!"

3:22	*And the scribes who came from Jerusalem*
	  said,
	    "Beelzebul has him!"
	  and

	"By the prince of demons he casts out demons!"
3:23	*And calling them to himself,*
	he spoke to them in parables:
	"How is Satan able to cast out Satan?
3:24	If a **kingdom** is divided **against itself**,
	that kingdom is not able to stand.
3:25	And if a **house** is divided against itself,
	that house will not be able to stand.
3:26	**And if Satan** stands up **against himself** and is divided,
	he is not able to stand, but is finished!
3:27	But absolutely **no one is able** to go into **the house of a strong man to steal his property**
	unless he *first* binds the strong man,
	and *then* plunders his house.
3:28	Amen, I say to you,
	All things will be forgiven men and women,
	sins and blasphemies, whatever the blasphemies may be;
3:29	but whoever blasphemes **against the Holy Spirit** will **not** have forgiveness ever,
	but is guilty of an eternal sin!
3:30	*(Because they had said, "He has an unclean spirit.")*
3:31	*And his mother and brothers came and, standing outside, they sent a message to him, calling him by name.*
3:32	*And a crowd was seated around him;*
	and they said to him,
	"Look! Your mother and your brothers are outside looking for you."
3:33	And he replied to them,
	"Who is my mother and who are my brothers?"
3:34	*And looking about at those who were seated in a circle around him,*
	he said,
	"Look at my mother and my brothers!
	For whoever does the will of God,
	that person is my brother and sister and mother."
4:1	*And again he began to teach alongside the sea.*
	And an enormous crowd moved toward him,
	so large that he got into a boat to sit on the sea,
	and all the crowd was on the shore next to the sea.
4:2	And he taught them many things in parables,

A Narrative Version of "Q"   57

	and he said to them in his teaching:
4:3	"Listen!
	The sower went out to sow seed.
4:4	And it happened that as he sowed
	some fell on the road,
	and birds came and ate it.
4:5	And other seed fell on rocky ground
	where it did not have much soil,
	and it sprang up quickly because it lacked a depth of soil,
4:6	and when the sun rose it burned,
	and because it did not have root, it withered.
4:7	And yet other seed fell into the thornbushes,
	and those bushes grew up and choked it,
	and it did not give fruit.
4:8	And other seeds fell onto good soil,
	and growing and increasing they gave fruit,
	and bore fruit thirtyfold and sixtyfold and a hundredfold."
4:9	And he said:
	"Whoever has ears to hear, let him hear!"
4:21	And he said to them:
	"Is the light brought to be placed **under the** measuring basket or by the bed?
	Is it not brought to be placed **on the lampstand**?
4:22	For a thing is not hidden
	except for the purpose of its being made manifest,
	nor is a thing made secret
	but that it should become clear.
4:23	If anyone has ears to hear, let him hear!"
4:24	And he said to them:
	"Understand what you hear!
	With the measure you use to measure
	will it be measured out to you
	and provided for you.
4:25	For,
	he who has,
	it will be given to him;
	and he who has not,
	even what he has will be taken from him."
4:26	And he said:
	"In this way is the kingdom of God

	like a man who should cast seed upon the soil
4:27	and would go to sleep and get up, day after day,
	and the seed should sprout and grow
	without the man's knowing how.
4:28	By itself the soil bore fruit,
	first the stalk,
	then the ear of grain,
	then the full grain within the ear.
4:29	But when the grain is ripe,
	immediately he sends out the sickle
	because the harvest has come."
4:30	And he said:
	"To what can we **liken the kingdom of God,**
	or in **what** parable are we to represent it?
4:31	It is like a **grain of mustard,**
	which when it is sown upon the soil,
	though smallest of all the seeds that are on earth,
4:32	yet when it is sown,
	rises up **and becomes** the largest of all the herbs
	and puts out large branches,
	so that **the birds of the air can settle** in its shade."
4:33	*And with many such parables did he speak "the word" to them,*
	according to their ability to "hear" it.
4:35	*And he said to them on that day toward evening,*
	"Let us go across to the other side."
4:36	*And leaving the crowd,*
	they took him in the boat, just as he was,
	and other boats were with him.
4:37	And a great squall of wind arose,
	and the waves spilled over into the boat,
	so that the boat was already filling.
4:38	But he was in the stern, sleeping on a pillow;
	and they wakened him
	and said to him,
	"TEACHER,
	do you not care that we are perishing?"
4:39	And having wakened,
	he rebuked the wind
	and said to the sea,

	"Be silent! Be still!"
	And the wind dropped
	and there was a great calm.
4:40	And he said to them,
	"Why are you fearful?
	Do you not yet have faith?"
4:41	And they were very much afraid
	and said to one another,
	"Who then *is* this,
	that even the wind and the sea obey him?"
5:1	*And they went into the region beyond the sea, into the territory of the Gerasenes.*
5:2	*And as he was getting out of the boat*
	a man with an unclean spirit came to meet him from the cemetery,
5:3	who had his home among the tombs;
	and no one was any longer able to bind him with a chain,
5:4	because he had many times been bound by fetters and chains,
	and the chains had been torn apart by him
	and the fetters, broken,
	and no one was strong enough to subdue him;
5:5	and night and day among the tombs and in the hills
	he was crying out and bruising himself with stones.
5:6	And seeing Jesus from a distance, he ran and knelt before him,
5:7	and crying out with a load voice he said:
	"What is there between me and you,
	JESUS, SON OF THE GOD MOST HIGH?
	I implore you by God, not to torment me!"
5:8	(*For he had been saying to him:*
	"*Unclean spirit, come out of the man!*")
5:9	And he asked him,
	"What's your name?"
	and he said to him,
	"My name is 'Legion,' because we are many."
5:10	And he continued many times to implore him not to send them out of the country.
5:11	Now, there was there near the hill a large herd of pigs feeding;
5:12	and they implored him, saying:
	"Send us into the pigs, so that we might enter into them."

5:13	And he allowed them.
	And coming out, the unclean spirits went into the pigs,
	and the herd rushed down the cliff into the sea,
	about two thousand in all, and they drowned in the sea.
	And they were afraid.
5:14	And those who were tending them ran away and reported it in the city and in the towns;
	and the people came to see what it was that had happened.
5:15	And they came to Jesus,
	and they saw the man who had been possessed sitting,
	clothed and sane, he who had had "the Legion,"
	and they were afraid.
5:16	And the witnesses described to them
	how it had happened to the possessed man and about the pigs.
5:17	And they began to implore him to go away from their territory.
5:18	*And, as he was getting back into the boat,*
	the man who had been possessed begged him, that he should be with him.
5:19	And he did not permit him,
	but said to him:
	"Go back to your home to your family,
	and report to them how much the Lord has done for you
	and how much he has had mercy on you."
5:20	And the man went away and began to proclaim in the Decapolis
	how much *Jesus* had done for him,
	and everyone wondered.
5:21	*And when Jesus had crossed again [in the boat] to the other side,*
	a huge crowd gathered together to him,
	and he was beside the sea.
5:22	And one of the leaders of the synagogue, Jairus, came
	and, seeing him, fell at his feet,
5:23	saying:
	"My little daughter is dying!"
	and implored him insistently to come and lay his hands on her so that she would be healed and live.
5:24	And he went with him
	and a large crowd followed him and crowded around him.

A Narrative Version of "Q"

5:25	And a woman who for twelve years had had a flow of blood,
5:26	and who had suffered much under many doctors, and who had spent everything she had and who had in no way been helped, but rather had gotten worse,
5:27	*having heard about Jesus,* *and having come up from behind in the crowd,* touched his garment;
5:28	for she had said: "If I could only touch his clothes, I'll be saved!"
5:29	And her flow of blood at once dried up and she sensed that she was healed of the illness.
5:30	And Jesus, aware that the power had gone out from him, turned around in the crowd and said: "Who touched my clothes?"
5:31	And his disciples said to him, "You see the crowd pressing in on you, and you ask, 'Who touched me?'"
5:32	And he was looking around to see who had done this thing.
5:33	But the woman, fearful and trembling, knowing what had happened to her, came and fell down before him and told him the whole truth.
5:34	He, however, said to her: "Daughter, your faith has saved you; go in peace, and be healed from your illness."
5:35	*While he was still speaking,* men came from the house of the leader of the synagogue, saying: "Your daughter is dead. Why still trouble the Teacher?"
5:36	But Jesus, overhearing the message, said to the leader of the synagogue, "Do not be afraid; just have faith!"
5:37	And he did not allow anyone to accompany him except Peter and James and John, James's brother.
5:38	And they went into the house of the leader of the synagogue,

	and he found an uproar, people both weeping and wailing loudly,
5:39	and as he entered he said to them,
	"Why are you making an uproar and weeping?
	The child hasn't died but is sleeping."
5:40	And they laughed at him.
	He, however, after putting everyone out,
	took the child's father and mother and those who were with him
	and went into where the child was;
5:41	and taking hold of the child's hand,
	he said to her,
	"Talitha koum" *(which is translated: "Little girl, I say to you, arise!")*.
5:42	And the little girl immediately got up and walked around, *(for she was twelve years old)*.
	And they were [immediately] astounded, in utter amazement.
5:43	And he repeatedly instructed them that no one should know about this,
	and he said to give her something to eat.
6:1	*And he went away from there,*
	and went into his hometown,
	and his disciples followed him.
6:2	*And on the sabbath he began to teach in the synagogue;*
	and many who were listening were astonished,
	saying,
	"From what source did these things come to this man?
	And how was wisdom given to this man,
	and how do such mighty works happen at his hands?
6:3	Is not this the carpenter, the son of Mary
	and the brother of James and Joses and Judas and Simon?"
	And they took offense at him.
6:4	And Jesus said to them:
	"A prophet is not without honor
	except in his hometown
	and among his own relatives
	and in his own house."
6:5	And he was unable to do any mighty work there,

A Narrative Version of "Q"

	except for a few sick persons whom he healed by a laying on of hands.
6:6	And he marveled at their lack of faith.
	And he traveled around the villages one by one, teaching.
6:7	And he called to himself [his disciples][27]
	and began to send them out, two by two,
	and he gave them power over the unclean spirits;
6:8	**And** he charged **them** that they should take nothing "on the way," but only a **staff**—
	no bread,
	no bag,
	no money in the belt—
6:9	but that they, wearing sandals, should also not put on two tunics.
6:10	And he said to them,
	"Whenever you enter a house,
	stay there until you leave from there.
6:11	**And if any** place **does not receive you** or listen to you,
	as you leave **from** there, **shake off** the dust from under **your feet,**
	as a witness against them."
6:12	And they went out
	and preached that people should change their lives,
6:13	and they cast out many demons,
	and they anointed many sick persons with oil and healed them.
6:30	*And the apostles came together to Jesus*
	and reported to him everything that they had done
	and everything they had taught.
6:31	*And he said to them,*
	"Come, you yourselves, alone into a deserted place, and get a little rest."
	For there were many people coming and going
	so that they didn't have a chance to eat.
6:32	*And they left in the boat for a deserted place, alone.*
6:33	*Yet many saw them leaving and recognized them,*
	and ran there on foot from all the cities,

---

27. The text's reference to "the Twelve" is taken to be a later narrowing of the focus, although there is, admittedly, no textual evidence to support such narrowing.

	and arrived before them.
6:34	*And when Jesus got out of the boat he saw a huge crowd, and his heart went out to them because they were like sheep without a shepherd, and he began to teach them many things.*
6:35	And with the hour already being late his disciples came to him and said:
	"The area is deserted and the hour is already late;
6:36	send them away so that they may go away into the fields and villages around here and buy themselves something to eat."
6:37	But he replied to them,
	"You feed them!"
	and they said to him,
	"Are we to go and buy two hundred denarii worth of bread in order to feed them?"
6:38	So he asked them,
	"How many loaves do you have? Go and see."
	And having found out, they said,
	"Five, and two fishes."
6:39	And he ordered them to have everyone recline in groups on the green grass.
6:40	And they reclined in groups by hundreds and by fifties.
6:41	And taking the five loaves and the two fishes, he looked up to heaven and gave thanks and broke the loaves into pieces and gave them to [his] disciples for them to serve the others, and he divided the two fishes among them all.
6:42	And everyone ate and was satisfied;
6:43	and there were broken pieces enough to fill twelve baskets, not to mention what was left from the fish.
6:44	And those who ate [the loaves] were 5,000 men.
6:45	*And he immediately made his disciples get into the boat and go ahead to the far side, toward Bethsaida, while he sent the crowd away.*
6:46	*And having said good-bye to them he went away into the hills to pray.*
6:47	*And when evening came*

| | the boat was in the middle of the sea |
| | and he was alone on land. |

6:48 And seeing that they were having difficulty rowing, for the wind was against them,
at about the fourth watch of the night he went to them, walking on the sea;
and he intended to pass by them.

6:49 But when they saw him walking on the sea,
they thought,
"It's a ghost!"
and they screamed;

6:50 for every one saw him and they were frightened.
But he at once spoke with them
and said to them,
"Have courage!
It is I.
Don't be afraid!"

6:51 And he climbed into the boat with them,
and the wind dropped,
and they were extremely astonished,

6:52 *for they had not understood the meaning of the loaves,*
but their comprehension was dulled.

6:53 *And when they had crossed over to land,*
they came to Gennesaret and anchored.

6:54 *And as they got out of the boat,*
the people at once recognized him

6:55 *and ran about that whole district*
and began to carry around on stretchers those who were sick to wherever they heard he was.

6:56 *And whenever he would go into a village or into a city or into the fields,*
they would place the sick in the marketplaces
and beseech him to let them simply touch the hem of his garment;
and as many as touched it were made well.

7:1 *And Pharisees and some of the scribes who had come from Jerusalem gathered together to him*

7:2 *and, seeing some of his disciples were eating bread with unclean hands*

7:3	*(that is, unwashed, for the Pharisees and all the Jews do not eat unless they carefully wash their hands, observing the tradition of their forefathers,*
7:4	*nor do they eat anything from the market without sprinkling, and there are many other things which tradition has them observe, washing cups and jugs and utensils [and beds])*,
7:5	the Pharisees and scribes questioned him: "Why do your disciples not follow the traditions of our forefathers, but eat bread with unclean hands?"
7:6	But he said to them, "Well did Isaiah prophesy about you hypocrites, as it is written: 'This people worships me with their lips, but their heart is far away from me;
7:7	in vain do they worship me, teaching doctrines which are the commandments of men,'
7:8	when, neglecting the commandment of God, you observe the commandment of men.
7:9	And he said to them, "How well you get around the commandment of God, in order to uphold your own tradition!
7:10	For Moses said, 'Honor your father and your mother,' and, 'Let the one who speaks ill of father or mother surely die';
7:11	but *you* say, If a man should say to his father or mother, 'Corban' *(that is, 'It's given')*, whatever help you would have had from me,'
7:12	you will no longer permit him to do anything for his father or his mother,
7:13	invalidating the word of God with your teaching which you hand on; and many such similar things do you do."
7:14	*And again calling the crowd to him,*

A Narrative Version of "Q"

       he said to them,
          "Everyone listen to me and understand!

7:15   There is nothing which goes into a man from outside him
       which can make him unclean;
       but the things which come out of a man are the things
       which make him unclean."

7:17   *And when he entered the house away from the crowd,*
his disciples asked him about the parable.

7:18   and he said to them,
       "So, are *you* also without understanding?
       Do you not perceive that
       'everything which goes into a man from the outside
       is unable to make him unclean,

7:19   because it does not go into his heart
       but into his stomach, and goes out down the drain?'
                       (thus making all foods "clean").

7:20   But he said:
       "What comes out of a person,
       that makes a person unclean;

7:21   for from within, out of a person's heart,
       come forth evil plans:
          immorality,
          theft,
          murder,

7:22   adultery,
          greed,
          malice,
          deceit,
          indecency,
          envy,
          slander,
          arrogance,
          folly;

7:23   all these evil things come out from within and make a
          person 'unclean.'"

7:24   *Then he got up and went from there into the region of Tyre.*
And entering a house, he wanted no one to find out;
but he could not escape notice!

7:25	*And* a woman who had heard about him and whose daughter had an unclean spirit
	came and fell at his feet;
7:26	(*The woman was Greek, a Syrophoenician by birth.*)
	and she asked him to cast out the demon from her daughter.
7:27	And he said to her,
	"Let the children first be satisfied,
	For it is not right to take the bread of the children and throw it to the dogs."
7:28	But she said in reply,
	"LORD,
	even the dogs under the table eat the crumbs of the children!"
7:29	And he said to her,
	"Because of this response, go home!
	The demon has gone out of your daughter."
7:30	And going away to her home
	she found the child lying on the bed
	and the demon gone out of her.
7:31	*And when he went back from the region of Tyre,*
	he went through Sidon to the Sea of Galilee through the region of the Decapolis.
7:32	*And* they brought to him a deaf person who could only speak with difficulty
	and they begged him to lay his hand on him.
7:33	And when he had taken him away from the crowd by himself,
	he put his fingers into the man's ears
	and he spat and touched his tongue,
7:34	and looking up to heaven he sighed
	and said to him,
	"Ephphatha!" (*Which means, "Be opened!"*)
7:35	And his hearing was opened up,
	and the cord of his tongue was loosed,
	and he spoke clearly.
7:36	And he ordered them not to say anything;
	but however much he ordered them,
	they instead proclaimed it all the more.
7:37	And they were incredibly astounded,
	saying,

"He does *everything* well!
he even makes the deaf hear and the dumb speak!"

8:1 *In those days,*
when there again was a large crowd that did not have anything
to eat,
he called his disciples
and said to them,

8:2 "I have compassion for the crowd
because they have been with me three days now,
and they don't have anything to eat;

8:3 And if I should send them home hungry,
they will grow weak on the way,
and some of them have come a long distance."

8:4 And his disciples responded:
"From what source could anyone be able to satisfy
these people with breads here in a wilderness?"[28]

8:5 And he asked them,
"How many loaves do you have?"
And they said,
"Seven."

8:6 And he commanded the crowd to sit down on the ground;
and taking them, he blessed and broke the seven loaves
and gave them to his disciples to serve,
and they set them before the crowd.

8:7 And they had a few small fish;
and having blessed them,
he said to serve these also.

8:8 And they ate,
and were satisfied,
and there were enough fragments left over to fill seven baskets.

8:9 And there were about 4,000 persons.
And he sent them away.

8:10 *And immediately getting into the boat with his disciples,*
he went into the region of Dalmanoutha.

8:11 *And* Pharisees went and began to argue with him,
seeking a sign from heaven on his behalf, testing him.

---

28. See Hugh Humphrey, "Jesus as Wisdom in Mark," *Biblical Theology Bulletin* 19 (1989): 48–58.

8:12	And, groaning from the depths of his soul
	he said,
	    "Why does this generation seek a sign?
	    Amen I say to you,
	    on no account will a sign be given to this generation."

8:13	*And leaving them, he again got into the boat and went to the other side.*
8:14	*And they had forgotten to take bread along,* *and* except for one loaf, they did not have any with them in the boat.

8:15	And he instructed them,
	    "Look!
	    Beware of the leaven of the Pharisees
	    and the leaven of Herod."

8:16	And they thought to themselves that they did not have breads.

8:17	And realizing it
	he said to them,
	    "Why are you thinking that you have no breads?
	    Do you not yet perceive or understand?
	    Are your minds closed?

8:18	Having eyes, do you not see and having ears, do you not hear? And do you not remember,
8:19	when I broke the five loaves for the 5,000, how many baskets full of fragments did you take?" They said to him, "Twelve."
8:20	"And the seven, for the 4,000, how many baskets full of fragments did you take?" And they said [to him], "Seven."
8:21	And *he* said to them, "Don't you *yet* understand?"
8:22	*And they came into Bethsaida.* *And* the people brought to him a blind man and urged him to touch him.
8:23	And taking the blind man's hand he led him out of the village; then, having spat on his eyes and laid his hands on him, he asked him,

	"What do you see?"
8:24	And looking up,
	he said,
	"I see men;
	I see them like walking trees."
8:25	Then again he laid his hands on the man's eyes,
	and the man opened his eyes wide and was well again,
	and he looked at everything clearly.
8:26	And he sent the man to his home,
	saying,
	"Do not even go into the village!"
8:34	*And calling the crowd to himself, with his disciples,*
	he said to them,
	"If any one wants to follow after me,
	let him deny himself completely
	and take **his cross**
	and follow me.
8:35	For **whoever** wants to save **his life,**
	will destroy it;
	but whoever destroys his life
	will save it.
8:36	For what does it profit a man to gain the whole world
	only to forfeit his life?
8:37	For what exchange can a person make for his life?
8:38	For whoever is ashamed of me and of my words
	in this adulterous and sinful generation,
	the Son of Man will also be ashamed of **him**
	when he comes in the glory of his Father with **the** holy
	angels."
9:1	And he said to them,
	"Amen I say to you:
	There are some standing here who will not taste death
	until they see the kingdom of God come in power!"
9:2	*And after six days Jesus took along Peter and James and John,*
	and he led them up onto a high mountain by themselves.
	And he was transformed before them,
9:3	and his garments became glistening, very white,
	such as no one on earth could bleach them.
9:4	And Elijah appeared to them, with Moses,

	and they were conversing with Jesus.

9:5	And in response,
	Peter said to Jesus,
	  "Rabbi,
	    it's a good thing we are here!
	    Let us make three shelters,
	    one for you,
	    and one for Moses,
	    and one for Elijah!"

9:7	And a cloud enveloped them,
	and a voice came out of the cloud,
	  "*This* is MY BELOVED SON!
	  Listen to *him!*"

9:8	And suddenly, looking around, they no longer saw anyone, but *only* Jesus alone with them.
9:14	*And coming to the disciples* *they saw a large crowd around them and scribes arguing* *with them.*
9:15	*And as soon as the whole crowd saw him, they were utterly* *amazed,* and ran up to him and greeted him.
9:16	And he asked them, "What were you arguing about with them?"

9:17	And a person from the crowd answered,
	  "TEACHER,
	  I brought my son to you with a dumb spirit;

9:18	and wherever it seizes him, it dashes him down,
	  and he foams and grinds his teeth and becomes rigid;
	  and I said to your disciples that they should cast him out,
	  but they were not able to do so."

9:19	And replying to them,
	he said,
	  "O unbelieving generation,
	  how long will I be with you?
	  How long will I put up with you?
	  Bring him to *me!*"

9:20	And they brought him to him. And seeing him, the spirit at once convulsed the man's son and falling to the ground, he rolled about foaming.

A Narrative Version of "Q"

9:21	And Jesus asked his father, "How long has he been like this?" and the man replied, "Since childhood;
9:22	And it often hurls him into fire and water in order to destroy him. But if indeed it is possible, help us and have compassion on us!"
9:23	And Jesus said to him, "'If it's possible...!' All things are possible to the person who has faith!"
9:24	At once the boy's father cried out and said, "I believe! Help my lack of faith!"
9:25	But Jesus, seeing that a crowd was gathering, rebuked the unclean spirit, saying to it, "Dumb and deaf spirit, I command you, come out of him and no longer enter into him!"
9:26	And crying out and convulsing many times, it came out. and he seemed like a dead man, so that many said "He's dead!"
9:27	But Jesus took hold of his hand and raised him up, and he stood up.
9:28	*And when he had entered a house* *his disciples privately asked him,* "Why were we not able to cast it out?"
9:29	And he said to them, "This kind is by no means able to come out except through prayer."
9:33	*And they came into Capharnaum.* *And when he was in the house,* he asked them, "What were you arguing about on the way?"
9:34	But they were silent, for they had been discussing among themselves on the way "Who is the greatest?"

9:35	And sitting down, he called the Twelve
	and said to them,
	   "If anyone wants to be first,
	   let him be last of all and servant of everyone."

9:36	And taking a child, he put the child in front of them and, embracing the child, said to them,

9:37	"Whoever receives one of these children in my name,
	   receives me;
	   and whoever **receives me,**
	   receives not so much me as **the one who has sent me."**

9:38	John said to him,
	   "TEACHER,
	   we've seen someone casting out demons in your name,
	   and we tried to stop him,
	   because he was not following us."

9:39	But Jesus said,
	   "Don't try to stop him,
	   for there is no one who is able to do a mighty work in my name
	   and able quickly to speak evil of me;

9:40	for he who is not against us, is for us!

9:41	For whoever would give you a cup of water on the ground that you are 'Christ's,'
	   amen I say to you,
	   'He will not lose his reward!'

9:42	And whoever is an occasion of sin to one of these little ones who believe in me,
	   it would be good for him instead if a donkey's millstone were put around his neck
	   and he were thrown into the sea.

9:43	And if your hand is an occasion of sin for you, cut it off;
	   it would be a better thing for you to go into life disabled
	   than with two hands to go out into hell, into the unquenchable fire.

9:45	And if your foot is an occasion of sin for you, cut it off;
	   it would be a better thing for you to go into life lame
	   than with two feet to be thrown into hell.

9:47	And if your eye is an occasion of sin for you, throw it away;

	it would be a better thing for you to go into life with one eye
	than with two eyes to be thrown into hell,
9:48	where their worm doesn't die
	and the fire is not put out.
9:49	For everyone shall be 'salted' with fire.
9:50	**Salt is a good thing;**
	but if salt should become tasteless,
	with what will you season it?
	You, have salt in yourselves,
	and live in peace with one another!"
10:1	*And setting out from there he went into the region of Judea around the Jordan;*
	and again a crowd ran up to him
	and, as he was accustomed to do,
	again he taught them.
10:2	*And* Pharisees came
	and asked him, testing him:
	"Is it permitted for a man to divorce his wife?"
10:3	Answering, he said to them,
	"What did Moses command you?"
10:4	But they said,
	"Moses allowed a man to write a certificate of divorce and to send her away."
10:5	And Jesus said to them,
	"On account of your hardened heart he wrote that commandment for you.
10:6	But from the beginning of creation
	Male and female he made them;
10:7	for this reason a man leaves behind his father and his mother
	[and joins himself to his wife]
10:8	and the two will be one body.
	(Thus they are no longer two, but rather one body.)
10:9	What therefore God has joined together, let not man separate!"
10:10	*And in the house again,*
	the disciples asked him about this.
10:11	And he said to them,
	"Whoever divorces his wife

	and marries another woman,
	commits adultery against her,
10:12	and if she, having divorced her husband,
	marries another man,
	she commits adultery."

10:13 *And people brought children to him for him to touch them; but the disciples rebuked them.*

10:14 But when Jesus learned of it, he was indignant and said to them,
> "Let the children come to me!
> Don't try to stop them,
> for the kingdom of God belongs to such persons.

10:15 Amen I say to you,
> whoever does not receive the kingdom of God like a child shall not enter into it."

10:16 And putting his arms around the children,
he blessed them
and laid his hands upon them.

10:17 *And as he was setting out on a journey,*
a man ran up to him and knelt before him
and asked him,
> "Good TEACHER,
> What shall I do so that I may inherit eternal life?"

10:18 And Jesus said to him,
> "Why do you call me 'good'?
> No one is good except one, God.

10:19 You know the commandments:
> You shall not murder,
> You shall not commit adultery,
> You shall not steal,
> You shall not bear false witness,
> You shall not defraud
> Honor your father and your mother."

10:20 But he said to him,
> "TEACHER,
> I have observed all these from my youth."

10:21 And Jesus, looking straight at him, liked him very much
and said to him,
> "There is one thing you don't have:

	Go, sell whatever you have and give to the poor,
	and you will have a treasure in heaven,
	and come, follow me."
10:22	But the man became gloomy at the teaching
	and went away distressed,
	because he had many possessions.
10:23	And looking around,
	Jesus said to his disciples,
	"How difficult it is for those who have possessions
	to enter the kingdom of God!"
10:24	The disciples, however, were amazed at his words.
	And Jesus, again responding,
	said to them,
	"Children,
	how difficult it is to enter the kingdom of God;
10:25	it is easier for a camel to pass through the eye of a needle,
	than for a rich man to enter the kingdom of God."
10:26	But they were even more overwhelmed,
	saying to themselves,
	"Then who can be saved?"
10:27	Looking straight at them,
	Jesus said,
	"With men it is impossible,
	but not with God,
	for everything is possible with God."
10:28	Peter began to say to him,
	"Look, *we* have left everything and followed you!"
10:29	Jesus said:
	"Amen I say to you,
	there is no one who has left home,
	or brothers or sisters
	or mother or father or children
	or fields
	because of me and because of the 'good news!'
10:30	who shall not receive a hundredfold now in this age,
	homes
	and brothers and sisters

	and mothers and children
	and fields,
	and eternal life in the age to come.
10:31	Many who are first, however, will be last,
	and the last, first."
11:11	*And he went into Jerusalem, into the temple;*
11:15	And, going into the temple
	he began to throw out the people who were buying and selling in the temple,
	and he upset the tables of the money changers and the seats of the dove sellers,
11:16	and he did not allow anyone to carry a utensil through the temple.
11:17	And he taught
	and said to them
	"Is it not written:
	'My house shall be called a house of prayer for all peoples'?
	But *you*, you have made it a robbers' cave!"
11:27	*And while he was walking about in the temple,*
	there came to him chief priests and scribes and elders,
11:28	and they said to him,
	"With what authority do you do these things?
	Or who has given to you such authority
	that you should do these things?"
11:29	But Jesus said to them,
	"I will ask you one question;
	answer me,
	and I will tell you with what authority I do these things:
11:30	Was John's baptism from heaven or from men?
	Answer me!"
11:31	And they debated among themselves,
	"If we should say
	'From heaven,'
	he will say
	'Why then did you not believe him?'
11:32	but if we should say
	'From men'...!"

A Narrative Version of "Q"

> *(They were afraid of the crowd,*
> *for everyone held John to have been a prophet.)*

11:33   And they answered
and said to Jesus,
> "We don't know."

So Jesus said to them,
> "Neither will I tell you with what authority I do these things!"

12:13   *And they sent to him some of the Pharisees and some of the Herodians*
to find a mistake in what he was teaching.

12:14   And they came and said to him,
> "TEACHER,
> we know that you are honest
> and do not bother yourself about anybody
> nor consider the outward appearance of persons,
> but in truth teach the way of God;
> is it permissible to give a poll tax to Caesar or not?
> Should we give or should we not give?"

12:15   But Jesus, knowing their hypocrisy,
said to them,
> "Why do you put me to the test?
> Bring me a denarius that I may see it."

12:16   And they brought one.
And he said to them,
> "Whose image is this, and the inscription?"

And they said to him,
> "Caesar's."

12:17   And Jesus said to them,
> "The things that belong to Caesar,
> give to Caesar;
> but the things that belong to God,
> give to God!"

And they were utterly amazed at him.

12:18   *And there came to him Sadducees,*
and *they* questioned him:

12:19   > "TEACHER,
> Moses wrote for us:

	If a man should die and leave behind a wife
	but not leave a child,
	that
	his brother should take the wife
	and should raise a family for his brother.
12:20	There were seven brothers;
	and the first took a wife,
	and when he died did not leave a family;
12:21	and the second one took her,
	and died, not leaving a family.
	So did the third, similarly.
12:22	And the seven did not leave a family.
	Last of all the wife also died.
12:23	In the resurrection [when they rise up],
	to which of them will she be a wife?
	For all seven had her as a wife."
12:24	Jesus said to them,
	"Isn't it because you know neither the scriptures
	nor the power of God that you are wrong?
12:25	For when they rise from the dead,
	they neither marry nor are given in marriage,
	but are like angels in heaven.
12:26	On the matter of the dead rising up,
	don't you know in the book of Moses,
	in the passage about the bush,
	how God said to him:
	'I am the God of Abraham,
	and [the] God of Isaac
	and [the] God of Jacob'?
12:27	He is not God of the dead, but of the living!
	You are *very* wrong."
12:28	*And one of the scribes approached, having heard their arguing,*
	and seeing that he had responded to them well,
	asked him,
	"Which is the most important commandment of all?"
12:29	Jesus answered:
	"The first is
	'Hear, O Israel,
	the Lord our God is one Lord,

A Narrative Version of "Q"

12:30	and you shall love the Lord your God with all your heart and with all your soul and with all your mind and with all your strength.'
12:31	The second is this: 'You shall love your neighbor like yourself.' There is no other commandment greater than these."
12:32	And the scribe said to him, "Quite right, TEACHER! You have correctly said He is one and there is no other before him
12:33	and to love him with all your heart and with all your understanding and with all your strength and to love the neighbor like oneself is far better than all the whole burnt offerings and sacrifices."
12:34	And Jesus, seeing that he had spoken with understanding, said to him, "You are not far from the kingdom of God." *And no one anymore dared to question him.*
12:37	*And the large crowd listened to him eagerly.*
12:38	*And* in his teaching he said: "Watch out for the scribes who like to walk around in long robes and who enjoy greetings in the marketplaces
12:39	and front seats in the synagogues and places of honor at dinners;
12:40	These men who devour the estates of widows and pray a long time for show, will receive a more severe condemnation!"
13:1	*And when he was coming out of the temple, one of his disciples said to him,* "TEACHER, look! What stones and what buildings!"

13:2	And Jesus said to him, "Are you admiring these grand buildings? There will not be left here a stone upon a stone that will not be pulled down."
13:3	*And when he was seated on the Mount of Olives, across from the temple,* Peter and James and John and Andrew asked him privately,
13:4	"Tell us, when will these things happen, and what is the sign that all these things are about to be accomplished?"
13:5	But Jesus began to say to them,[29]
13:8	"Nation will rise up against nation, and kingdom against kingdom, there will be earthquakes in various places, there will be famines; a beginning of the birth pangs are these things.
13:12	And brother will deliver up brother to death and a father a child, and children will turn against parents and be the cause of their death.
(13:13)	But he who endures until the End, that person will be saved.
(13:14)	Then let those who are in Judea flee to the mountains,
13:15	let the person on the roof not go down nor go in to take anything from his house,
13:16	and let the person in the field not turn back to the things behind to take his coat.
13:17	But woe to women who are pregnant and to women who are nursing in those days;
13:19	For those days will be an affliction

---

29. The text I give here represents the materials in the third person that form a "narrated discourse. They are markedly apocalyptic in character and...have a coherence of their own." See Humphrey, *"He is Risen!"* 117. The materials in the second person in Mark 13 tone down the urgency of the third-person materials and are best understood as representing a later stage of the redaction of Mark's Gospel.

	of such a kind as has not happened since the beginning of the world
	that God created until now and never will be.
13:20	And if the Lord had not cut short the days,
	not a single person would be saved.
	But for the sake of *the elect* whom he chose,
	he has shortened the days.
13:22	For false christs and false prophets will arise
	and they will present signs and wonders
	in order to lead astray, if possible, *the elect*.
13:24	But in those days,
	after that affliction,
	the sun will be darkened,
	and the moon will not give its light,
13:25	and the stars will be falling from the sky,
	and the powers in the heavens will be shaken.
13:26	And then they will see the SON OF MAN coming on clouds
	with much power and glory!
13:27	And then he will send out the angels
	and he will gather together [his] *elect* from the four quadrants,
	from the end of the earth to the end of the sky.
13:30	Amen, I say to you,
	This generation will not pass until all these things happen!
13:31	Heaven and earth will pass away,
	but my words will not pass away.
13:32	However, concerning that day or the hour,
	no one knows,
	not the angels in heaven,
	nor THE SON,
	but only the Father.

The Community Reflected by Mark's Narrative Version of Q

It is evident that Mark's literary activity was not the simple one of jotting down the memories of Peter. When Mark assembled the *chreiae* attributed to Jesus,[30] he did so in the context of a narrative with a central character; secondary characters like Peter, Andrew, James, John, the crowd, the various Jewish religious groups; and a sequence of events building to an eschatological climax that is at once a challenge to "the elect" and a threat to those outside that community. That narrative, as we have seen, echoes the themes of the Q tradition. Precisely because it *is* a narrative, however, it allows us to see reflected in its details the concerns of the evangelist and, one supposes, of the community that sustained him and for whom he was their voice.

The community implied by Mark's narrative version of Q appears to have a sense of themselves as "the elect"[31] of the "kingdom of God," an eschatological reality[32] soon to be consummated by the appearance of the Son of Man.[33] As the elect, they have chosen to follow Jesus' ethical principles of "love God" and "love your neighbor,"[34] which for them is the essence of the will of God as expressed in the Hebrew Scriptures.[35] The use of the Septuagint in allusions and arguments suggests a community for whom these citations from the Jewish Scriptures would have had authority. Indeed, the question of "authority" is an acute one for them: *whose* authority are they to follow? It is readily apparent that it is *God's* will that they must follow,[36] and that God has granted Jesus authority

---

30. Papias used the phrase πρὸς τὰς χρείας and may have been acknowledging, through a term in ancient rhetoric, a specific literary form of anecdote in which the essential elements are the identification of a well-known person and a noteworthy comment. There are many of these in Mark (1:17; 2:8–11, 17, 19–22, 25–28; 3:23–29; 4:2–9, 21–32; 5:34; 6:4, 10–11; 7:6–15, 18–23; 8:34–9:1; 9:23, 31, 39–50; 10:5–9, 14–15, 18–21, 23–25, 39–40, 42–45; 11:17, 29–30; 12:17, 38–40; 13:2; 14:18, 24–25), and almost every one occurs in the narrative version of Q. Sharyn Dowd has persuasively reported extensively on the Greco-Roman rhetorical devices parallel to Mark (*Reading Mark: A Literary and Theological Commentary on the Second Gospel* [Macon, GA: Smyth & Helwys, 2000]). There is an a priori reason, therefore, to be open to finding the paradigm of *chreia* in Mark. Indeed, the more the picture of the author of Mark's Gospel becomes that of an individual, educated in the forms of Hellenistic rhetoric and affluent enough to afford the expense of writing materials time and again, the more the alleged connections to the John Mark of Jerusalem seem to wither.
31. Mark 13:20, 22, 27.
32. Mark 1:15.
33. Mark 13:26–27.
34. Mark 12:29–31.
35. Mark 12:34.
36. Mark 3:35.

to teach[37] what the will of God requires in this eschatological "kingdom of God." This community is scathing in its rejection of hypocrisy in following God's will, attributing that hypocrisy stereotypically to the Jewish religious leaders in a series of controversies that erupt when Jesus enters into the heart of the Jewish world, Jerusalem (11:11–12:34). The triumphant tagline at the end of 12:34, "And no one anymore dared to question him," expresses the community's confidence that when it is a matter of interpreting the Jewish religious writings, Jesus gave the authoritative interpretation. Mark's community responded to the leaders' hypocrisy by insisting that the two principles centered on love of God and love of neighbor are "far better than all the whole burnt offerings and sacrifices" (12:33), which are hypocritically performed when love is absent.

This suggests, further, that Mark and his community, at this stage of the composition of Mark's Gospel, are still in dialectic with a contemporary Jewish community, one that has raised the objection that God's will is expressed definitively in their Scriptures. At this early period the Markan community not only countered that opposition with the narration of these controversies over the interpretation of Scripture, but also, as in the Q material, with the presentation of Jesus as the one *chosen* by God to be the Holy One of God,[38] the one acknowledged by the demonic world as the "Son of God,"[39] on whom God's Spirit rests. These motifs are announced at the very beginning of Mark's narrative version of Q, and the consequence is that Jesus can act with an "authority" *unlike* that of the scribes (1:22) and chief priests and elders (11:28). Jesus is *"the Teacher"*[40] of God's will. (Absent in this narrative version of Q, as in Q itself, is any heightening of reflection on the nature of Jesus; indeed, Jesus' question in 10:18, "Why do you call me 'good'?" and his remark, "No one is good except one, God," has to be the nadir of "low Christology.")

---

37. While the theophany at the baptism of Jesus was not a public event, the reader of Mark's Gospel, and the Markan community itself, would have understood that event of the conferring of the Spirit upon Jesus as a conferring of a mission to teach (see that exact understanding in 1:38) and to teach authoritatively. Again, this understanding is explicitly communicated to the representative disciples, Peter, James, and John, in the transfiguration account when the mandate given in the theophany is to "listen to" Jesus (9:7), after which they "see" *only* Jesus" (9:8).
38. Mark 1:24.
39. Mark 3:11.
40. Disciples and nondisciples alike refer to Jesus or address him as "Teacher": Mark 4:38; 5:35; 9:17; 9:38; 10:17; 10:20; 12:14, 19, 32; 13:1.

One senses also that the community reflected by Mark's narrative version of Q sought to apply the fundamental principles centered on love in an egalitarian community, seeking to live by the prayer Jesus had taught his disciples. Even though the text does not show the disciples as praying, it several times presents Jesus as involved in prayer, and the motifs of the "Lord's Prayer" are implicit throughout this text.

"*Our Father...*" The disciples understand that they are "brothers and sisters" of Jesus (3:34), who know that God is their "Father" (13:32), the final word of the document.

"*who art in heaven...*" Heaven is where God is (1:10–11; 6:41; 7:34; 8:11; 10:21; 11:30–31; 12:25).

"*hallowed be thy name!*

"*Thy kingdom come!*

"*Thy will be done!*" These three phrases constitute synonymous parallelism. God's name will be hallowed, when his kingdom comes, and that will happen when God's will is done by all. The opening of this text announces the nearness of the kingdom of God (1:1–15) and the change of commitment and allegiance (1:15; 10:24) that is necessary for that to happen. The kingdom is near when the principles of love of God and love of neighbor are realized (12:34), when people do the "will of God" (3:35). The parable of the Sower, following immediately after 3:34, describes the need for the hearer personally to provide a place for that "seed"/love to "bear fruit" (4:1–8).

"*on earth as it is in heaven.*" The kingdom of God on earth is to be a restoration of the Garden of Eden, before human disobedience, when God's will prevailed among humankind.

"*Give us this day our daily bread....*" Bread in Mark is clearly a metaphor (6:52; 8:17–21) for an insight or understanding of what should be the correct response to Jesus, to God's will as expressed through Jesus. What one prays for each day is that understanding of what God's will requires in the events of the day, an understanding of how people are to bring to expression the twin principles of love of God and love of neighbor, just as Jesus had done in numerous instances in this narrative (e.g., in the cycle of stories in 5:1–20, 21–24 with 35–43, 24–34; and 7:24–30, 31–36; Jesus' "compassion" is explicitly in focus in 6:34 and 8:2).

And lead us not into temptation but deliver us from evil.... If the principle of love of neighbor moves people toward each other into an egalitarian community, the realities of the world create distinctions that move people apart. Sel*fless*ness is difficult to maintain in the face of sel*fish*ness, and we can see a focus on self rather than on the neighbor in the pursuit of material things that become an extension of the self. Hence, the parable of the Sower reports that some quite receptive individuals are like seed choked by thornbushes (4:7),[41] and Jesus observes how hard it is for "a rich man to enter the kingdom of God" (10:22-25). The ethic Jesus teaches is not something accomplishable by mere human effort but only with God's assistance (10:27), and for that reason one must pray to God in this fashion.

And so the community reflected by Mark's narrative version of Q is a largely Jewish-Christian one, seeking to live the egalitarian ethic of love it believes is the essence of God's will for humankind and previously announced in the Jewish Scriptures, but not being practiced by its contemporary Jewish counterpart. To this description one should add a sense of eschatological urgency. The community thinks of itself as baptized by the same Spirit (1:8) as was conferred on Jesus and mandated to carry on the same work as Jesus (3:14), as they in fact do (6:12-13, 30; 9:18). The text expresses that urgency in several ways. It begins with Jesus' challenge to "repent" and change because "the present age has reached its end and the kingdom of God has come near" (1:15). It was announced with Jesus' breaking down the power of Satan in the wilderness temptations (1:12-13) and with his ongoing work of overcoming the demonic world. Indeed, the strong man's house *is* being plundered in these last days begun by Jesus and continued in the community's work (3:23-27; 6:13). The one *un*forgivable sin then and now is to confuse the authority and power of the Spirit present in Jesus and in the community with that of Beelzebul's (3:22, 29-30)! How much longer these last days will continue even "the Son" (Jesus) does not know; only "the Father" knows (13:32). On that note this strongly eschatological narrative ends. It is left for those who are among the elect to "endure until the end" (13:13).

The fact that the Hebrew Scriptures are cited in their Septuagint form, combined with the frequent employment of the Hellenistic genre of *chreia* and the awkward geographical references used — all these suggest an author and a community in the Hellenistic world outside Palestine.

---

41. The explanation of the parable of the Sower (Mark 4:14-20), a later element in the composition of our present text of Mark's Gospel, describes these persons as "those who hear 'the word,' and the worries of the age and the deception of wealth and the craving for other things, creeping in, choke off 'the word,' and it becomes 'fruitless.'"

Even the approval of the Syrophoenician woman's entreaty (7:24–30) and Jesus' venturing into the Decapolis (7:31–37) to make the deaf hear and the dumb speak (7:37) involve the Hellenistic world. The same applies to the earlier episode of Jesus' healing of the possessed man of Gerasa, when Jesus told him, "Report... how much the Lord has done for you and how much he has had mercy on you" (5:19).

It is not really possible to determine more specifically where and for whom Mark wrote this narrative version of the Q tradition. My earlier comments about the appropriateness of Alexandria as a possible context remain valid for the description of the community given here.

Chapter Three

The Passion Narrative in Mark

Introduction:
The Account of Jesus' Death and Resurrection

The purpose of this chapter is twofold: (1) to indicate a narrative component of the Gospel of Mark whose focus and themes are entirely different from what has been identified as Mark's narrative version of Q; and (2) to indicate that this second narrative layer in Mark's Gospel has also been subject to substantial elaboration before it came to the final form it has in our present text of Mark's Gospel. Our focus here is what scholars call the Passion Narrative (PN), a detailed account of Jesus' final days in Jerusalem.

Here I contend that in the materials that now comprise the PN (14:1–16:8) it is possible to discern one basic account and two substantial elaborations of that, as well as materials that were, presumably, added as the present text of the Gospel was composed. Identifying the PN as distinctively different from the QN emphasizes that the present text of the Gospel of Mark has resulted from *at least* the conjoining of these layers of composition and suggests also a way of resolving the seemingly contradictory patristic witness traced in chapter 1 (above).

A Second Early Christology Reflected in Mark

The *present* text of Mark's Gospel, the Gospel of Mark as we have it today, emerged at a point in early Christianity when the memories about Jesus had already taken distinctly different forms. On the one hand, the reconstruction of that early collection of Jesus' sayings known as Q portrayed a prophetic figure, the last emissary of divine Wisdom, who had come to Israel to prepare the people to live righteously before God in a new kingdom soon to be brought into being. Jesus' word had authoritative power and could heal and give life. What was important was to know Jesus' teaching. How Jesus' life would end was not important and apparently not ever in focus. This reconstruction of Q is tentatively dated to the first or second decade after the death of Jesus because it has not yet moved to that higher level of christological affirmation that would be evident later in the century. By that time Jesus is not simply the agent of Wisdom, but also the presence of God, whose death on the cross can have redemptive value, taking away the sins (plural) of humankind.

The themes of the narrative layer in Mark reflecting that view are simple and are parallel to the perspective of the Q material, as we have seen: Jesus follows the career of the Baptist and is the one on whom the Spirit of God rests. Consequently, his coming announces the eschatological reality of the kingdom of God, where men and women do the will of God. As the Spirit-led Holy One of God, he knows what the commandment of God is and can distinguish it from the commandment of men, so that he is the essential "righteous man," the true "Son of God." He speaks "the word" with an authority confirmed by the casting out of the unclean spirits; indeed, his mission is to go from town to town preaching, teaching, and casting out demons. In this material the references to the Son of Man are as the future agent who will bring the "elect" into that kingdom, functioning as the vindicator of Jesus. Many of the alleged Markan parallels to the Q material appear in this layer of material. After a series of conflicts over interpreting the law of Moses, this narrative layer of material not surprisingly (since future vindication is an aspect of the Q material as well) ends with an eschatological sermon in Mark 13. Its narrated discourse is in the third person. As in Q, there is no anticipation of the death of Jesus, whom all (except the demonic world) know as "The Teacher."

And yet, on the other hand, we can find evidence for another theology of early Christianity in the letters of Paul, which also date from that formative period of the 50s. They relate virtually nothing of the historical activity of Jesus; instead, they focus on the consequences of God's having broken into human history to raise Jesus from the dead, thereby confounding all human wisdom and disclosing our precious judgments as the foolishness they are in God's sight (cf. 1 Cor 1).[1] Yet resurrection cannot occur without there first having been a death, and so Paul's theology centers on the death and resurrection of Jesus. Paul is anxious,

---

1. When Paul refers to Jesus as "our Wisdom" in 1 Cor 1:30, the context of the preceding text clearly shows that it is a reference to an ethic, a way of life, and not a reference to Jesus' being either the agent of God's Wisdom or Wisdom itself.

moreover, to emphasize that his theology is grounded on what he had himself first learned from those who had instructed him in the Christian tradition; what was central to Paul is what he had himself been taught: that "Christ died..., and that he was buried, and that he was raised,... and that he appeared to Cephas" (1 Cor 15:3-4).[2]

By contrasting Jesus with Adam, Paul portrayed the significance of God's raising Jesus from the dead to accomplish a radically new beginning for *all* of humankind. "For just as by the one man's [Adam's] disobedience the many were made sinners, so by the one man's [Jesus'] obedience the many will be made righteous" (Rom 5:19). The force of the contrast rests in the way Adam was thought of in the rabbinic tradition, so that Paul could speak of Adam as "a type of the one who was to come" (Rom 5:14), meaning Jesus.

> Adam... stands for the real unity of mankind in virtue of his creation. There is also another factor. The nature of Adam's creation is made the basis of the duty of love, equality and peace among men.... Gen. 5.1 teaches that all men are the offspring of him who was made in the image of God.[3]

This idea of all subsequent generations of men and women being in solidarity with their progenitor enabled the idea that Adam's sin could become the occasion of death for all after him, and that the obedience of the one man, Jesus Christ, could bring reconciliation with God.[4] Jesus' obedience unto death has reversed the alienation from God that began with Adam's disobedience and expulsion from the Garden of Eden.

These perspectives Paul had earlier expressed with a slightly different emphasis in 1 Cor 15:21-23, 45-49. There he had explicitly referred to Jesus as "the last Adam" (15:45), and the corporate solidarity of all men and women, first with Adam and then with Jesus, is clear in 15:48-49.[5] In this context, however, it is not the death of Jesus that is in focus but the resurrection of Jesus, without which the death of Jesus would have no meaning. The first Adam brought death; the last Adam became a source of life for all who "belong to Christ" (15:23) because

---

2. Scripture from Paul's Epistles follow NRSV; other quotations are my own translation unless otherwise indicated.
3. W. D. Davies, *Paul and Rabbinic Judaism: Some Rabbinic Elements in Pauline Theology* (New York: Harper & Row, 1967), 55. For a fuller statement, see 52-57.
4. Ibid., 52.
5. W. D. Davies believes that these perspectives lie behind the idea of the one body of Christ (ibid., 55).

by his resurrection from the dead he became the "first fruits" of the final, eschatological gathering of the elect.

When the material of 1 Corinthians is aligned with the material in Romans, it becomes clear that Paul sought to express theologically the significance of Jesus' death for all of humankind through the contrast of Jesus, the last/second Adam, with the Adam portrayed in Genesis. And the explanatory text of Rom 5:19 provides the fundamental basis for God's having raised Jesus from the dead: it was an approval of his *obedience*. Adam's disobedience in the Garden of Eden was obvious; God had established the moral order at the very beginning by saying that everything was permitted ("You may freely eat of every tree of the garden" [Gen 2:16]) but one ("of the tree of the knowledge of good and evil you shall not eat" [2:17]). Adam's deliberate choosing to disobey a requirement of God's will made him the paradigm of all human endeavors to "become like God." Paul asserts that it was Jesus' radical obedience, even to the will of God for him that he should die, that makes Jesus the paradigm of all who would have life. Disobeying God's will brings "death" in the sense of alienation from God; obedience to God's will brings "life" in being reconciled with God.

It is precisely this focus that Paul approves when he cites the hymnic fragment in Phil 2. The context for the citation is ethical, an enjoining of the Philippians to "be of the same mind," and to "do nothing from selfish ambition or conceit, but in humility regard others as better than yourselves" (2:2–3); in this selflessness they make true community possible. So Paul asks that they have the same mind "that was in Christ Jesus,

> who, though he was in the form of God,
> did not regard equality with God as something to be exploited,
> but emptied himself, taking the form of a slave,
> being born in human likeness.
> And being found in human form,
> he humbled himself and became obedient to the point of death —
> even death on a cross. (2:5–8)

The contrast here is clearly between the first man, who was "in the form of God" but wanted to become like God, and Jesus, who emptied himself, humbled himself, and "became *obedient* to the point of death — even death on a cross." Verse 9 says "*Therefore* God also highly exalted him," approving Jesus' radical obedience to the will of God for him, even that he should die, by raising him from the dead.

And so we have three texts from the early Christian world reflected in the Pauline letters and written within three decades of the death of Jesus, all three emphasizing the significance of Jesus' giving of himself, even unto death, death as a revelation of the radical obedience to God's will that God will approve with resurrection/exaltation/reconciliation. To provide a cosmic and universal dimension for that significance, Paul makes the contrast between Adam, "who is a type of the one who was to come" (Rom 5:14), and Jesus, the last Adam; in that contrast there is a corporate solidarity of all those who "belong" to each respectively.

We find, therefore, that there were two, apparently distinct, directions in remembering Jesus: the authoritative teacher of God's will (Q) and the obedient Christ whom God raised from the dead. Each apparently could exist without explicit reference to the other. And when we turn to the present text of Mark's Gospel, it is possible to discern the same two directions of thought, but artfully woven together (see chap. 5, below). Mark's Gospel is a literary composition that underwent a number of revisions, each of which reflects specific characteristics and each of which has left inconsistent traces in the framework.[6]

There is reason to believe, then, that what we find in the present text of 14:1–16:8 is that second and distinct narrative layer, focused on that other early Christology reflected in Rom 5; 1 Cor 15; and Phil 2. What we find in the Markan texts of the betrayal, passion, death, and resurrection of Jesus is a *narrative* statement of this Christology, as we shall see, in the form of that narrative *assumed by* the passion predictions of 8:31; 9:31; and 10:33–34.

The Characteristic Features of Mark 14:1–16:8

If the unified section of 8:27–10:45 (where the three passion predictions occur) is left aside for the time being, then what the reader or hearer of the *present* text of Mark recognizes is a significant change in the manner in which the story of Jesus is narrated. The Jesus of Mark 13 — who spoke with authority about the End and the judgment by the Son of Man, who *will* come to save the elect — disappears from view. In the material that begins at 14:1, there is *no* emphasis upon Jesus' authority, *no* instances of miracles or healings, *no* reactions of amazement by the

---

6. There were blocks of material like the PN, of course, but also diverse materials reflecting changing perspectives concerning Jesus, what Jesus did, the disciples, the Twelve, and discipleship.

crowds, *no* demonic recognitions or casting out of demons, *no* preaching of individual righteousness that will lead to eternal life in the kingdom of God. In other words, the story with which the Gospel began — of Jesus, agent of God's Wisdom, proleptic presence of a future judge known as the Son of Man — is abandoned.

Instead, the characteristic features of the narrative that begins at 14:1 concerns the story of a law-observant Jew (he intends to celebrate the Passover, 14:12–16), *aware of God's will* for him that he be betrayed and put to death (14:13–16, 18, 20–21, 24–25, 27, and especially 32–42), and *obedient to it* (14:32–42!), who refers to himself as the Son of Man (14:21, 41). He is tragically betrayed by one of his own and deserted by his closest disciples, yet his obedience unto death as "the King of the Jews," or "Christ," leads to his being raised by God from the dead. This narrative exposes a clearly different set of interests.

The Outline of the Earliest Passion Narrative within Mark 14:1–16:8

We can easily discern the major elements of the framework fashioned in order to narrate the story of Jesus' betrayal by Judas, his last moments with his disciples, and his arrest at the wishes of the high priests and scribes; the passion predictions in 8:31 and 10:33–34 are concise and succinct summaries of,[7] and hence presuppose the existence of, the narrative account now embedded in 14:1–16:8.

As Donald Senior declared in 1984, "Contemporary biblical scholarship is divided over exactly how the passion story developed."[8] A decade later Raymond Brown's review of scholarship on a Pre-Markan Passion Narrative[9] judged the issue to be "almost evenly divided on whether or not to posit the existence of the pre-Marcan PN(s)."[10] What we speak of here as the "presupposed" PN summarized by the passion predictions is the account Mark knew and would incorporate in chapters 14 and 15. In

---

7. H. M. Humphrey, *"He is Risen!" A New Reading of Mark's Gospel* (New York: Paulist Press, 1992), 126.
8. D. Senior, *The Passion of Jesus in the Gospel of Mark* (Passion Series 2; Wilmington, DE: Glazier, 1984), 9.
9. R. E. Brown, *The Death of the Messiah: From Gethsemane to the Grave; A Commentary on the Passion Narratives in the Four Gospels* (Anchor Bible Reference Library; 2 vols.; New York: Doubleday, 1994), 1:53–57.
10. Ibid., 1:54.

our judgment Mark himself has first and creatively made the transition from an orally preached account[11] to a *narrative*.[12]

	Markan Passion Predictions		Passion Narrative
8:31	9:31	10:33–34	
"Son of Man"	"Son of Man"	"Son of Man"	
"must"	"will be"	"will be"	14:10–52
"suffer many things"	"delivered"	"delivered" to the "chief priests and scribes"	
"be rejected by the elders and chief priests and scribes"	"into the hands of men"	"they will condemn him to death"	14:53–15:1
		"and deliver him to the Gentiles"	15:2–39
		"They will mock him" "spit upon him" "scourge him"	15:16–20
"be killed"	"be killed"	"kill him"	

Those outlines in the passion predictions do not mention some of the material in Mark's final three chapters, and when we omit that material we find a simple, straightforward account, the final three items of which parallel Paul's tradition in 1 Cor 15:3–4:

- Jesus/Son of Man is to be betrayed (Mark 14:1, 10–11)
- and handed over to chief priests, elders, scribes (14:43–50)
- and then handed over to (Pilate) (15:1).
- There he is interrogated, mocked, and scourged (15:12–20) ⎫
- before being crucified (15:25–32). ⎬ As KING OF THE JEWS
- He *died* (15:33–37) ⎭
- and is *buried* (15:42–46)
- and is *raised* (16:1–6, 8), leaving an empty tomb.

The simplest of the passion predictions, 9:31, may reflect the simplest of kerygmatic proclamations underlying the narrative in 14:1–16:8: "the

---

11. I agree with Raymond Brown that there was a "strong likelihood that Mark was in continuity with a preached tradition about the death of Jesus and...elements of sequence in that preached tradition, e.g., from 1 Cor 11:23; 15:3–5," in ibid., 1:53.
12. For a review of the larger issue of pre-Markan sources, cf. the review by W. R. Telford, "The Pre-Markan Tradition in Recent Research (1980)," in *The Four Gospels 1992: Festschrift Frans Neirynck* (ed. F. van Segbroeck et al.; Bibliotheca ephemeridum theologicarum lovaniensium 100; Louvain: Leuven University Press, 1992), 693–723.

Son of Man is to be betrayed into human hands, and they will kill him, and three days after being killed, he will rise again" (NRSV).

The narrative that subsequently elaborated that simple kerygmatic proclamation, however, is probably not now recoverable from our present text. What we now find in the present text of Mark is narrative dramatizing and theologizing: Dramatizing, because Mark highlights the circumstances of one of his own disciples betraying Jesus to show its tragic ignominy (14:12–50); and theologizing, because Jesus' death as "King of the Jews" is set into Jewish expectations of "the Christ" (14:61; 15:32), and because the overall narrative of the death of the obedient Son of Man reflects the second-Adam Christology of Phil 2 and Rom 5:18–19, especially in Mark 14:32–42 (the scene in the Garden of Gethsemane) and 14:62.

Mark 14:62 is particularly interesting. The verse has three parts, linked together by the simple conjunction "and." The first part of 14:62 expresses the clear focus of the PN; Jesus is identified as the "Christ" who is going to be put to death. He is *also* the "Son of the Blessed One," implicitly the "son" who calls God "Father" in the Gethsemane narrative and to whom he is obedient even to the acceptance of his having to die; the early second Adam Christology invoked by Paul in Phil 2:9–11 is thereby called to mind.

The second part of 14:62, "*and* you will see the Son of Man at the right hand of the Almighty" continues that Christology by affirming exaltation for the "son" who had made himself "obedient to the point of death" (Phil 2:8). The hymn in Phil 2:5–11 clearly makes the contrast between the disobedience of God's first son, Adam, and his second "son," Jesus. Jesus thus becomes the exemplar of what God intended Adam to be and so could be understood as the *true* son of Adam, or "bar Adam," or "son of (the) man." And the hymn continues in Phil 2:9 to proclaim the exaltation of that obedient son, "therefore God has also exalted him," just as 14:62b adds that sense of exaltation for the "son" of 14:62a.

The first part of 14:62 is, therefore, entirely consistent with the focus of the PN and the second part provides the theological interpretation early Christianity gave to the death of Jesus.[13]

---

13. Only because the third part of 14:62 has been attached, "and coming with the clouds of heaven," has the reference to the Son of Man been given the sense of a future, apocalyptic judge. Clearly the third part of 14:62 is an addition to the earlier text in 14:62a-b. When this

The Dramatizing of the Betrayal in Mark 14:1, 10, 12–42

The narrative opens in 14:1 with a succinct identification of those responsible for Jesus' death and sets it against the background of the Passover. The introductory ῏Ην δέ, rare in Mark, indicates a clear transition to new material as it sets the material that follows against an explicit temporal reference (the Passover) and reintroduces characters (the high priests and the scribes) who had not been in the narrative for some time.[14] Moreover, their intention "to arrest and kill [Jesus] in some cunning way" (πῶς αὐτὸν ἐν δόλῳ κρατήσαντες ἀποκτείνωσιν) is put in the position of climax in this introductory verse and thereby governs all the material that follows.[15] The narrative continues in 14:10. There the simple succession indicated by Καί is extended into an element of the framework by (re)introducing Judas into the story of these events[16] and by making connection back to the "high priests" of 14:1. Just as 14:1–2 spoke of arresting Jesus "in some cunning way" and made a temporal reference ("not during the feast"), so also 14:10–11 speaks first of Judas's betrayal and then makes a temporal reference ("an opportune moment").

> Now the Passover and the feast of Unleavened Bread was in two
>   days,
> and the chief priests and scribes were looking for a way
> to arrest and kill him in some cunning way,
> for they said,
>   "Not during the feast, lest there be a riot of the people."
>   (14:1–2)
> And Judas Iscariot, who was one of the Twelve,

---

addition was made cannot be determined; it is, however, an addition consistent with other modifications made to assimilate QN and PN.

14. Although Mark's early chapters frequently mentioned the scribes, they had last been mentioned at 12:38; the high priests had been rarely mentioned in the first 13 chapters of Mark (8:31; 10:33; 11:18), and 11:27 was the last reference to them before 14:1.

15. Mark 14:3a certainly introduces a new geographical reference ("in Bethany"; "in the house of Simon the leper") that serves as a transition to the material in Mark 14:3b–9. This material, however, does *not* develop the focus of the narrative set in 14:1 (the intention to kill Jesus) but looks *beyond* the death of Jesus to the time when the "good news" is preached throughout the world. Since the material in 14:3–9 deals with Jesus' being buried without the usual anointing (see Mark 16:1), it appears to be *intrusive* here; if the narrative were to proceed from 14:2 directly to 14:10, its omission would never be noticed. Mark 14:1–30 is paralleled by the text of John 13:1–38 in 11 specific instances; the absence of this material in John (John 13:1–2//Mark 14:1, 10) further supports the probability that Mark 14:3–9 is a later intrusion into the PN assembled by Mark.

16. The only previous mention of Judas was as part of the list of the Twelve at 3:19.

went to the chief priests in order to betray him to them.
When they learned of it, they were glad and promised to give him money,
and he watched for an opportune moment to betray him.
(14:10–11)

After this brief sketching of the persons involved in bringing Jesus to his death and of their intentions, the narrative then begins to specify the time and manner of Jesus' betrayal more exactly. Mark 14:12 continues the succession of subordinate scenes introduced with Καί (14:1a, 10, and now 12), followed by a new and explicit temporal reference: "on the first day of the feast of unleavened bread, when they sacrifice the paschal lamb," a transitional phrase that picks up the references of 14:1a. This transitional seam introduces a scene that extends to 14:16, where the last word "Passover" (πάσχα) forms an inclusion with the two instances of the word in 14:12; in both verses the instances of οἱ μαθηταί reinforce the inclusion. Moreover, the content of this pericope is narrated in a series of short phrasings, each introduced by καί.

Mark 14:17 narrows the time frame even more when καί is followed by a new and explicit temporal reference and by a change of scene as Jesus rejoins the disciples (ἔρχεται). This change of scene is the setting for the first of a series of scenes centered on Jesus' betrayal by Judas. In 14:17–25 Jesus announces the betrayal (14:18) and underscores its ignominy ("one of *you*," v. 18; "one of *the Twelve,* dipping in the dish with me," v. 20; "Better for him if that man had not been born," v. 21) and its finality (vv. 22–25).

Transitional verses in 14:26–27 prepare both for the move to Gethsemane and for Jesus' betrayal being God's will, anticipated in a prophecy and shortly to be realized.

Mark 14:32 accordingly continues the change of scene begun in 14:26. In the Garden of Gethsemane two developments occur: Jesus' acceptance of Judas's betrayal as God's will (14:32–41, esp. v. 41) *and* his second identification of his betrayer ("He who betrays me approaches," v. 42).

Thus, in what appears to be a concentric organization of materials, we find five episodes:

- "The Teacher" plans a last, "Passover" meal (14:12–16).
- Jesus, "Son of Man," predicts betrayal (14:17–21).

- This "eucharistic" meal will be last before the kingdom of God: "Amen" (14:22–25).
- Jesus, "shepherd," predicts betrayal by the Twelve; Peter says "never!" (14:26–27).
- Jesus, the "Son" (calls God "Father"), accepts the will of God for him as "Son of Man" since "the hour has come" (14:32–42).

Nevertheless, the scenes in 14:12–42 in no way deal with the "kingdom of our father David" (11:10) or with Jesus as "the King of the Jews (15:1–32)." Jesus *the Son of Man* knows the plan laid out for him by God (14:13–16), anticipating his own betrayal (14:17–21) and the way his own disciples will be "scandalized" and will abandon him (14:26–31) as well as that the meal with his disciples will be his last with them (14:22–25). Indeed, in the Garden of Gethsemane scene, Jesus becomes the model of obedience to God's will. Thus, when Jesus knows that his very human effort to change God's will for him was for naught, he accepts it and goes to meet his fate as the true "Son of Man," Bar Adam, a NEW Adam obedient unto death (Phil 2): "Get up!" he says, "let's go!" (14:42).

The transitional, temporal reference in 14:43a moves to the narration of the actual betrayal by Judas in 14:42–50. The prophecy of Zech 13:7, quoted in 14:27, is still in view; it intensifies the tragedy when the "striking" of the shepherd takes the form of a kiss by his close friend. And surely Jesus' words in 14:49 are meant to refer back to and call to mind that prophecy, realized by the Judas kiss and the abandonment of Jesus by *all* his disciples in 14:50, and even by the young man (14:51–52).

And so, the betrayal of Jesus by Judas has been in focus from 14:1–2, 10–52. This dramatic, extensive narrative of betrayal finds its succinct expression in the first part of the predictions in 9:31; and 10:33–34.[17]

The Dramatization of the Rejection of Jesus

The passion predictions of 8:31 and 10:33 specifically attribute the rejection of Jesus to the chief priests and scribes and elders (8:31). Mark 10:33 adds: "They will condemn him to death and hand him over to the Gentiles, and they will ridicule him and spit on him and scourge him." These summary remarks provide an outline for the materials in 15:1–32.

---

17. Although there is a marked similarity among the predictions of 8:31, 9:31, and 10:33, the implication of betrayal is not present in 8:31; the more general sense that Jesus "must suffer many things" may have been chosen precisely because it was the first prediction.

The narrative succinctly summarized by those predications then turns to a series of scenes (14:53–65;[18] 15:2–5, 6–15, 16–20, 21–27, 29–32) that focus on Jesus as "the Christ," "the King of the Jews." The title "King of the Jews" appears conspicuously in five of these scenes (15:2, 9 and 12, 18, 26, 32). Enclosing these five scenes are corresponding scenes (14:53–65; 15:29–32) in which the high priest and scribes reject Jesus (cf. 14:53, 55 with 15:15, 31). In 15:29 Mark emphasizes the balancing of these two scenes by repeating the charge against Jesus in 14:58, that he "would pull down the temple in three days." And in these two scenes also, Mark replaces the title "King of the Jews" by the more appropriate (given the context) "Christ," which is then extended, first in 14:61 by the phrase "the Son of the Blessed One" and then in 15:32 by the phrase "the King of Israel."

In the Johannine version of the account of Jesus before Pilate, the five scenes are easily recognizable[19] because of the inside/outside pattern of the scenes that center on the ironic tragedy of Roman soldiers mocking Jesus. In the Markan account, however, the thematic emphasis is on Jesus being rejected. It first appears in his rejection by the Jewish religious authorities in 14:53–65, and it also appears in that closing scene of 15:29–32: the taunting of the high priests and the scribes that the crucified Jesus should come down from the cross "so that we might see and believe" expresses their conviction that he cannot do so. Their unbelief is clear. And Mark further emphasizes and heightens that theme of Jesus being rejected by his own people in what appears as the central scene in his concentric pattern, 15:12–15. There "the crowd," which had already rejected the replacement of Barabbas for Jesus in 15:11, now cries out "Crucify him!" not once but twice. Mark has unified the theologically elaborated materials in 14:53–15:32, therefore, both by their apparently concentric[20] structure and by their focus on Jesus being rejected as the

---

18. The trial before the high priest (Mark 14:55–65) serves as the context for the tradition about Peter's denial in 14:54, 66–72, which completes this development begun in 14:29–31; if 14:29–31 is secondary to *its* context, then 14:54, 66–72 are secondary here also.

19. Cf. R. E. Brown, *The Gospel according to John XIII–XXI: Introduction, Translation, and Notes* (Anchor Bible 29A; Garden City, NY: Doubleday, 1970), 857–59.

20. The elements of the framing scenes in Mark 14:53–65 and 15:29–32 are strikingly parallel. Both have the priests and scribes present, jeering. Both refer to the allegation that Jesus said he would "pull down the temple and build it in three days." And both employ the primary designation of "the Christ," then modified by an explanatory phrase. Moreover, the five instances of "the King of the Jews" strongly suggest an organization of materials centered on the third usage and on the rejection of Jesus by the cries from the "crowd": "Crucify him!"

"Christ," the "King of the Jews," both by the Jewish religious leaders and by the "crowd"[21] itself.

While some have asserted that the present text of Mark's Gospel is interested in presenting Jesus as "Messiah,"[22] Mark's text here only awkwardly sustains that interest. This instead is traditional material focused on Jesus' own people rejecting "the King of the Jews," and it explains the legal basis for the death of Jesus, a twin focus entirely absent from the early sections of the Gospel narrative.[23]

The Death and Burial of Jesus; and the Resurrection...?

The predictions in Mark 8:31; 9:31; and 10:33–34 moved quickly from Jesus' being "killed" to his being "raised," and Paul's tradition in 1 Cor 15 moved equally quickly from Jesus' having "died" to being "buried" to being "raised." The chronology employed here, focusing as it does on the circumstances surrounding Jesus' death, includes the account of his death in 15:33–37 and his burial in 15:42–46.

The passion predictions all close with the triumphant assertion that the Son of Man will rise after three days, and some proclamation of Jesus' resurrection surely followed the accounts of his death and burial. Nevertheless, one cannot be so confident that the account of the empty tomb in 16:1–8 was the form that proclamation originally took.[24] The narrative in 15:40–41 and 15:47–16:8 introduces motifs absent otherwise in this chronology (discipleship by women,[25] vv. 40–41; discipleship

---

21. The narrative version of Q portrayed the "crowd" quite differently. It was always approving of Jesus, seeking him out, even if in "wonder" and "amazement."
22. Thus, most recently, "Mark stresses this title [Messiah] as a description of Jesus.... The density of key terms in 1:1 prepares the reader for the dramatic unfolding of the whole work, which revolves around the proper description of Jesus as Messiah and Son of God." J. R. Donahue and D. J. Harrington, *The Gospel of Mark* (Sacra Pagina; Collegeville, MN: Liturgical Press, 2002), 60.
23. The five scenes in Mark 15:2–32 are themselves perhaps an expansion of an earlier, simpler chronology. Their apparent concentric arrangement and the prominence of the "King of the Jews" title, missing elsewhere and unprepared for, are suggestive of their being a composition elaborating a simpler narrative.
24. Reginald Fuller maintains that the tradition about Jesus' resurrection was at first proclaimed and only later narrated in stories centered on the empty tomb or the appearances to disciples. See R. H. Fuller, *The Formation of the Resurrection Narratives* (New York: Macmillan, 1971), 48, 66–67.
25. In the narrative of Jesus' betrayal, passion, and death, Mark has not earlier presented the motif of women disciples. Since it has not appeared anywhere else in the Markan traditions, Mark has to introduce the women by name.

in Galilee,[26] v. 41; fear and amazement,[27] 16:5, 6, 8). Hence, it may not have been in the traditional material known by Mark, summarized in the predictions, and then incorporated into the present text of Mark.

One Final Observation

The narrative layer identified here is at least earlier than some stage of our present text of Mark; this is clear not only from the passion predictions that presuppose it, but also from the evidence of the explanatory glosses provided in 15:10, 22, 34, and 42. These glosses show that this was recognized as an earlier block of material needing to be edited to make it Gentile-friendly, as it were, by translating or explaining Jewish customs or Hebrew phrasing.

Secondary Materials in Mark 14:1–16:8

The characteristic features described above are indicated by the summarizing Passion Predictions (8:31; 9:31; 10:33–34) and also cohere with the early Christology reflected in Phil 2 and Paul. Therefore, some materials in Mark 14:1–16:8 can be identified as secondary because they are intrusive or do not fit with the prevailing focus. I account for these in the composition history of Mark (see chap. 5, below).

The Anointing in Bethany (14:3–9)

This episode is deemed secondary for several reasons. (1) The episode focuses not on Jesus or his betrayal but on the woman and portraying her as a model of discipleship. (2) The anticipation of a future time when "the good news" is preached throughout the world breaks away from the focus on the time of the betrayal and passion of Jesus. (3) The narrative flow from 14:1–2 to 14:10 would be seamless if this episode were omitted.

The Prediction of Presence in Galilee (14:28)

The transitional phrasing in 14:26 moves Jesus and the disciples to the Mount of Olives and serves to introduce Jesus' prediction of the disciples' reaction, "All of you will be scandalized" (14:27), which in turn is seen as the realization of prophecy. The reaction of Peter in 14:29 continues

---

26. The focus of the PN has been on Jesus. The new focus on discipleship in Galilee as a faithful discipleship distracts from the angelophany and its proclamation that Jesus "is risen!"

27. These themes are characteristic of the narrative version of Q rather than of this narrative of the obedient Son of Man.

the focus on being "scandalized," and 14:50 gives the final element of this: "And everyone abandoned him and fled." Thus, the prediction of a resurrection appearance in this context is jarring and seems to be placed here solely to anticipate the statement of 16:7.

The Failed Discipleship of Peter (14:29–31, 54, 66–72)

Since the main narrative focus here is to recount the story of how Jesus was the obedient Son (of Man), these passages dealing with Peter's confident pledge of discipleship and sad failure to live up to his pledge appear to be secondary. They do, however, illustrate the full extent of Jesus' prediction in 14:27 that "all" the disciples, even Peter, would be scandalized.

The Reaction of the Centurion (15:38–39)

Since the main narrative in 14:1–16:8 is on what happens to Jesus, the centurion's exclamation is intrusive because it is interpretive. Moreover, because it is a "centurion" who, solely, reacts with faith, Mark deliberately contrasts that reaction to the preceding reactions by the passersby in 15:29, the high priests and scribes in 15:31, and the bystanders in 15:35. And finally, the "Son of God" appellation has been out of focus in this narrative (14:1–16:8), where the focus has been on the "Son of Man."

The Return to Galilee (16:7)

This verse is clearly secondary because it assumes the secondary material of 14:28. The focus on the future and on the rehabilitation of Peter and of the disciples — these are other motifs for which the preceding narrative has not prepared.

The Earlier Passion Narrative in Mark 14:1–15:46

14:1   *Now, the Passover and the Feast of Unleavened Bread was in
            two days,
        and the chief priests and scribes were looking for a way
        to arrest and kill him in some cunning way,*
14:2   *for they said,
            "Not during the feast, lest there be a riot of the people."*
14:10 *And Judas Iscariot, who was one of the Twelve,
        went to the chief priests in order to betray him to them.*

14:11	When they learned of it, they were glad	
	and promised to give him money	
	and he watched for an opportune moment to betray him.	
14:12	*And on the first day of the Feast of Unleavened Bread,*	
	when they sacrifice the paschal lamb,	
	his disciples said to him,	
	"Where do you want us to go and prepare for you to eat the Passover meal?"	
14:13	And he sent two of his disciples	
	and said to them,	
	"Go into the city,	
	and a man will meet you carrying a jar of water;	
	follow him,	
14:14	and wherever he enters, say to the master of the house,	
	'The TEACHER says,	
	Where is my guest room,	
	where I may eat the Passover meal with my disciples?'	
14:15	And he will show you a large upstairs room set and ready;	
	and there prepare for us."	
14:16	And the disciples left	
	and went into the city	
	and found it just as he had told them,	
14:17	*And when it was evening, he came*	*with the Twelve.*
14:18	And while they were at table and eating,	
	Jesus said,	
	"Amen I say to you,	
	One of you will betray me,	
	who is eating with me."	
14:19	And they began to be upset	
	and to say to him one after another,	
	"It's not me, is it?"	
14:20	But he said to them,	
	"It's one of the Twelve, one dipping in the dish with me.	
14:21	On the one hand, THE SON OF MAN goes	
	as it is written concerning him,	
	but on the other hand, woe to that man	
	through whom THE SON OF MAN is betrayed!	
	Better for him if that man had not been born!"	
14:22	And while they were eating, he took bread,	

	and having given thanks, he broke it
	and gave it to them
	and said,
	"Take! This is my body!"
14:23	And taking a cup, he gave thanks
	and gave it to them,
	and they all drank from it.
14:24	And he said to them,
	"This is my blood of the covenant
	which is being shed for many;
14:25	Amen I say to you,
	No longer will I ever drink of the fruit of the vine
	until that day when I will drink it new
	in the kingdom of God."
14:26	*And when they had sung a hymn,*
	they went to the Mount of Olives.
14:27	And Jesus said to them:
	"All of you will be scandalized,
	because it is written,
	'I will strike the shepherd,
	and the sheep will be scattered.' "
14:32	*And they went to a place called Gethsemane,*
	and he said to his disciples,
	"Sit here while I pray."
14:33	And he took along Peter and James and John with him,
	and he began to be utterly dismayed
	and to be much distressed,
14:34	and he said to them,
	"My soul is sad unto death;
	remain here and watch."
14:35	And going on a little, he fell to the ground
	and prayed that, if possible, the hour might pass from him,
14:36	and he said,
	"Abba, Father,
	everything is possible to you;
	take this cup away from me!
	But, not what I will,
	but what you will."
14:37	And he came and found them sleeping

	and he said to Peter, "Peter, why are you sleeping? Are you not strong enough to stay awake one hour?
14:38	Stay awake and pray, lest you enter into temptation; while the spirit is eager, the flesh is weak."
14:39	And again he went and prayed, saying the same thing.
14:40	And again he came and found them sleeping, for their eyes were heavy, and they did not know how to answer him.
14:41	And he came a third time and said to them, "Are you going to sleep and rest on and on? Enough! The hour has come. Behold THE SON OF MAN is betrayed into the hands of sinners.
14:42	Get up! Let's go! Behold, he who betrays me approaches."
14:43	*And at once, while he was still speaking,* Judas (one of the Twelve) appeared, and with him a crowd with swords and clubs from the chief priests and scribes and elders.
14:44	Now the one who betrayed him had given a signal to them, saying, "He is the one I kiss, seize him and lead him away securely."
14:45	*And he immediately went and approached him,* saying, "Rabbi!" and he kissed him with a show of affection.
14:46	The men, however, laid hands on him and seized him.
14:47	One of those present drew his sword and struck the servant of the high priest and took off his ear.
14:48	Jesus reacted and said to them, "Have you come out, as against a robber, to arrest me with swords and clubs?

14:49	Daily I was among you, teaching in the temple, and you did not arrest me; Well! Let the scriptures be fulfilled!"
14:50	And everyone abandoned him and fled.
14:51	*And there followed along with him* a certain young man, wearing a linen garment over his naked body, and they seized him;
14:52	but he left behind the linen garment and fled, naked.
14:53	*And they led Jesus away to the high priest, and all the chief priests, elders and scribes gathered.*
14:55	But the chief priests and the whole Sanhedrin were looking for evidence against Jesus in order to put him to death, and they could not find any.
14:56	For there were many false witnesses against him, yet their testimony did not agree.
14:57	And some rose and gave false witness against him, saying,
14:58	"We heard him say, 'I will pull down this temple made by hands, and in three days, I will build another not made by hands.'"
14:59	And not even their testimony was the same.
14:60	And the high priest stood up in the midst of them and questioned Jesus, saying, "Are you not going to answer anything? What is it these men are testifying against you?"
14:61	Yet he was silent and did not answer anything. Again the high priest questioned him and said to him, "Are you THE CHRIST, THE SON OF THE BLESSED ONE?"
14:62	But Jesus said, "I am, and You will see the Son of Man sitting at the right hand of the Almighty

	and
	coming with the clouds of heaven."
14:63	The high priest, however, tore apart his tunic
	and said,
	"What need do we still have of witnesses?
14:64	You have heard the blasphemy!
	How does it look to you?"
	All the others then judged him to be deserving of death.
14:65	And some began to spit upon him
	and to blindfold his face
	and to strike him
	and say to him,
	"Prophesy!"
	and the servants treated him to slaps.
15:1	*And very early in the morning,*
	the chief priests held council with the elders and scribes and the whole Sanhedrin,
	and they bound Jesus in chains and led him away
	and handed him over to Pilate.
15:2	And Pilate questioned him,
	"Are you THE KING OF THE JEWS?"
	But he answered and said,
	"*You* say."
15:3	And the chief priests accused him of many things.
15:4	But Pilate again questioned him, saying,
	"Are you not going to answer anything?
	See how many things they accuse you of!"
15:5	But Jesus still answered nothing, so that Pilate wondered.
15:6	Now, at each feast he used to set free for them one prisoner whom they chose.
15:7	There was one called Barabbas in prison among the revolutionaries
	who had committed murder in the uprising.
15:8	And the crowd went up and began to ask him to act according to custom for them.
15:9	Then Pilate responded to them,
	saying,
	"Do you want me to release to you THE KING OF THE JEWS?"

15:10 *(For he knew the chief priests had handed him over because of envy.)*
15:11 But the chief priests agitated the crowd
so that he should release to them Barabbas instead.
15:12 Then Pilate again responded
and said to them,
"What then [do you want] me to do
with [the one called] THE KING OF THE JEWS?"
15:13 They again cried out,
"Crucify him!"
15:14 Then Pilate said to them,
"Why? What evil thing has he done?"
But they cried out louder than ever,
"Crucify him!"
15:15 Then Pilate, wanting to satisfy the crowd, released to them Barabbas,
and handed Jesus over to be crucified,
after he had had him scourged.
15:16 *The soldiers then led him away into the palace* (that is, the Praetorium),
and they summoned the whole cohort.
15:17 And they dressed him in purple;
and they twisted together a crown of thorns
and put it on him
15:18 and began to salute him,
"Hail, KING OF THE JEWS."
15:19 and they struck his head with a reed
and spit on him,
and kneeling they paid homage to him.
15:20 And when they had ridiculed him, they took the purple off him
and dressed him in his clothes
and led him out in order to crucify him.
15:21 *And they pressed into service a certain passerby,* Simon of Cyrene,
who was coming in from the country, the father of Alexander and Rufus,
to take up and carry his cross.

15:22	And they brought him to the "Golgotha" place
	(which translated is "Place of a Skull").
15:23	And they gave him wine spiced with myrrh, which he did not take.
15:24	And they crucified him
	and divided up his garments among themselves,
	casting lot over them to see who would take what.
15:25	Now it was the third hour when they crucified him.
15:26	And the inscription of the charge against him read,
	"THE KING OF THE JEWS."
15:27	And with him they crucified two robbers, one on the right side and one on his left.
15:29	*And those who walked by abused him,* shaking their heads and saying,
	"Well, well, well!
	You who would pull down the temple and build it in three days,
15:30	save yourself by coming down from the cross!"
15:31	And the high priests, too, jeering among themselves and with the scribes,
	said,
	"He saved others;
	himself he is not able to save!
15:32	Let THE CHRIST, THE KING OF ISRAEL, come down from the cross now,
	so that we might see and believe!"
	And those who were crucified with him taunted him.
15:33	*And when it was the sixth hour, a darkness came over the whole earth until the ninth hour.*
15:34	And in that hour Jesus called out with a loud voice,
	"Eloi, eloi, lema sabachthani?" *(which translated is, My God, My God! Why have you forsaken me?)*
15:35	And some of the bystanders, when they heard it,
	said,
	"Look! He's calling Elijah!"
15:36	Then someone ran and filled a sponge with sour wine
	and put it on a reed and offered it to him to drink,
	saying,
	"Let us see if Elijah will take him down!"

15:37	But Jesus, having let out a loud cry, gave up his spirit.
15:40	Now there were women watching from a distance, among whom were Mary the Magdalene and Mary the mother of James the Younger and Joses, and Salome,
15:41	who when they were in Galilee had followed him and served him, and many other women who had gone up with him to Jerusalem.
15:42	*And since it was by now becoming evening,* seeing that it was the day of preparation *(the day before the Sabbath)*,
15:43	Joseph of Arimathea, an influential member of the Sanhedrin, who was himself eagerly awaiting the kingdom of God, went and had the courage to approach Pilate and petition for Jesus' body.
15:44	But Pilate wondered whether he was already dead, and summoning the centurion, he asked him if he had died already.
15:45	And learning from the centurion that he had, he granted the body to Joseph.
15:46	And having bought a piece of fine linen, he took him down and wrapped him in the linen and placed him in a tomb which had been hewn from rock; and he rolled a stone against the entrance to the tomb.
15:47	*But Mary the Magdalene and Mary the mother of Joses saw where he was put.*
16:1	*And when the Sabbath was over,* Mary the Magdalene and Mary the mother of James, and Salome bought spices in order to go and anoint him.
16:2	*And very early on the first day of the week,* they went to the tomb when the sun had risen.
16:3	And they said to one another, "Who will roll away the stone from the entrance of the tomb for us?"
16:4	And looking up, they saw that the stone had been rolled away, *for it was very large.*
16:5	And when they went into the tomb,

	they saw a young man sitting on the right side, wearing a long white robe.,
16:6	But he said to them,
	"Do *not* be amazed!
	You're looking for THE CRUCIFIED JESUS OF NAZARETH.
	He has risen!
	He is not here!
	Look at the place where they put him!"
16:8	And they went out and fled from the tomb,
	for a trembling and a bewilderment possessed them,
	and they said nothing to anyone,
	for they were afraid.

The Community Reflected by Mark's Earlier Passion Narrative

The text of that PN assumed by and summarized in the passion predictions of 8:31; 9:31; and 10:33–34 offers some grounds for describing the community for whom it is of interest. That community seems to be largely, if not entirely, *Jewish Christian;* for them, the references to the Passover and the Feast of the Unleavened Bread in 14:1 and 14:12 are suggestive and meaningful contexts for the drama that unfolds in the PN. Although the motif of a new "exodus" is not developed as it will be in Luke's Gospel, and the motif of Jesus as the "Lamb of God" is not developed as it will be in the Gospel of John, these motifs may well be recognized by a follower of Jesus whose life as a Jew has been influenced by the annual celebration of these events. To put it another way, specifying contexts of the Passover and Feast of Unleavened Bread has no meaning, either temporal or symbolic, to a non-Jew, but they do have both temporal and possibly symbolic meaning to a follower of Jesus with experience of or empathy toward the Jewish tradition.

Moreover, it would appear that the explanations in 15:16, 22, and 34 presuppose an earlier version of the text. In that earlier version the references to "the palace" and "Golgotha" and the citation of "Eloi, eloi…" apparently did not need explanation because a Jewish audience understood them, but a later, non-Jewish audience would not.

Mindful of the assertion of Dieter Georgi that Judaism was not a monolithic entity, but that a variety of Jewish groups existed and that individuals could easily "migrate" from one to another, it is nonetheless clear that in Mark's PN the community reflected there has already made a choice. The self-identity of that group as a Jewish-Christian group is clear. It understands itself as standing over against the Jewish religious leaders mentioned explicitly in 14:1, 43, 53, 55, 60–61, 63; and 15:1, 3, 11, 31. Those Jewish religious leaders had brought "false witness" (14:57) against Jesus, something even the high priest acknowledges in 14:60. Even Pilate knew that "the chief priests had handed him over because of envy" (15:10). Those same "high priests...with the scribes" (15:31) mocked the crucified Jesus. Indeed, those "chief priests accused" Jesus (15:3), further "agitated the crowd" to demand that Barabbas be released (15:11), and presumably continued stirring up the crowd to insist that Pilate yield to their cry: "Crucify him!" (15:13–14).

The Jewish profile of the community reflected by Mark's PN is also supported by the interpretation of Jesus' acceptance of his suffering and death as obedience to the will of God. The narration of the scene in the Garden of Gethsemane has as its single focus the portrayal of Jesus as embracing the will of God for him that he should die. It stands in somewhat awkward tension with the preceding narrative, where Jesus has shown his knowledge of the events that would unfold (14:13–16, 18, 25), and there is earlier no shadow of hesitation on Jesus' part, no trace of an awareness that those events could be subject to a reprieve. And yet that is what Jesus is seen asking for in the Gethsemane scene, a reprieve: "Father, everything is possible to you; take this cup away from me!" (14:36). But the request is really only a prelude to the affirmation of Jesus' acceptance of the Father's will: "But, not what I will, but what you will" (14:36). And *three* times the request is made; three times Jesus hears no reprieve being granted; thus, the climax to the scene demonstrates Jesus actively moving to accomplish the Father's will that he die: "Enough! The hour has come. Behold the Son of Man is betrayed into the hands of sinners. Get up! Let's go!" (14:41–42). The humbling of himself in obedience, even "unto death"—praised in Phil 2:8 as a reversal of the disobedience of Adam—is the sole purpose of Mark 14:32–42. It portrays Jesus, then, as the perfectly righteous one, who acknowledges the true dominion of God over all creation. Later, when he begins the recitation of Ps 22:1 in Mark 15:34, "Eloi, eloi, lama sabachthani," he begins a psalm that influenced the narration of the passion account,[28] but which ends with that proclamation of God's dominion over all: "For dominion belongs to the LORD" (Ps 22:28 NRSV). Jesus' final words begin a recitation of a psalm, the very essence of which is the acknowledgement of God's dominion over all and the assurance that he would reverse the fate of the afflicted. Early Christianity would capture this obedience of Jesus under the titles of "the Holy One" and "the Righteous One" (Acts 3:14).

In the Diaspora, where the Wisdom of Solomon would provide a context for hearing the passion account, the "righteous one" is also the "son of God," and people would hear the use of that phrase in 14:61 (and 15:39) as entirely consistent with the portrayal of Jesus as the perfectly obedient, righteous one. Indeed, the remark about Pilate knowing that the chief priests handed Jesus over "because of envy" (15:10) is reminiscent of the comment that "through the devil's envy death entered the world, and those who belong to his company experience it" (Wis 2:24 NRSV).[29] And the motif of the high priests and the scribes taunting the crucified Jesus is also reminiscent of the uncomprehending derision of the unrighteous in Wis 4:17–18 and 5:4. To those for whom the Wisdom of Solomon was a religious text, these parallels and the overall portrayal of the "two ways" of Jewish Wisdom literature in Wis 2 would have been lenses through which to interpret Mark's passion account and the Gethsemane scene in particular.

And so the community reflected by Mark's passion account was not only Jewish Christian but also one that embraced Jesus as a model of one's complete giving of self, even unto death. The emptying of self (*kenosis*) in obedience to God's will, so in focus in Phil 2 and in Mark 14:32–42, is here embraced by the community responsible for this account as its fundamental wisdom. All its members are, in effect, to say as Jesus did: "Let's go!" (14:42). The ethic is one of *kenosis*, which puts the emphasis upon what must be done at the present moment in order to accomplish God's will; that is wisdom and defines the truly wise person.

A consequence of this analysis is to say that the community responsible for the passion account was here *not apocalyptic* in its orientation,

---

28. Mark surely intended the account of dividing the garments and casting lots for them (15:24) as an allusion to Ps 22:18.

29. The remark is an allusion to Adam's disobedience, as is clear from the phrasing that immediately precedes this: "God created us for incorruption, and made us in the image of his own eternity" (Wis 2:23), a clear reference to Gen 1:27. Hence, we must understand the remark about death's entering the world as referring to the curse upon Adam (Gen 3:19).

as the community behind the narrative version of the Q material had been. The thrust of the eschatological emphases in the narrative version of Q reaches its climax there with the ending apocalyptic discourse in Mark 13; the focus is on the future and on the future consequences of one's present actions. We can find none of that emphasis in the passion account. Even Jesus' response to the high priest in 14:62, "You will see the Son of Man sitting at the right hand of the Almighty," is consistent with our analysis here. This is a statement of the complete confidence of the righteous one that God will not abandon him but that he will instead have God's companionship. It expresses the theme of Ps 22, which influenced the passion account: "The afflicted shall eat and be satisfied; those who seek him shall praise the LORD! May your hearts live for ever!" (22:26 RSV). It also reflects the confidence of the righteous in the Wisdom of Solomon: "The righteous live forever, and their reward is with the Lord; the Most High takes care of them" (5:15). The only apocalyptic shadowing to be found in Mark's passion account is with the phrasing appended to 14:62, "coming with the clouds of heaven," an apparent effort to invoke an allusion to the Son of Man in Dan 7; it is, however, not part of the preceding phrase but linked to it with "and." Jesus' response in 14:62 has actually three separate and distinct parts: an initial "I am," followed by "You will see the Son of Man sitting at the right hand of the Almighty," followed by "coming with the clouds of heaven." Stringing these parts together with "and" indicates a pasting together of phrasings and not one single response. The allusion to "the Son of Man" in 14:62 can be seen as consistent with the theme of the New Adam, the perfectly Righteous One as illustrated by his radical obedience to the Father's will, which permeates the passion account. Hence, to advance this verse as evidence for an apocalyptic perspective rests solely,[30] and weakly, on the appended phrasing that draws upon Dan 7. Offsetting that and showing that reference to the clouds of heaven to be uncharacteristic of this passion account is the fact that from its beginning the "Son of Man" has been introduced as "the Teacher" (Mark 14:14 and 21). A wisdom perspective prevails from start to finish, and the essence of that wisdom is the kenotic emptying of one's self to fulfill the will of God.

---

30. One also recognizes in the passion account the absence of the cosmic dimension notable in the narrative version of Q; there is no reference to Satan nor to the dawning of the apocalyptic kingdom in the casting out of the demonic.

We can also recognize that the community reflected by Mark's passion account has no explicit openness toward nor interest in including non-Jews into its ranks. Mark 15:39 has been left out of this reconstruction, but even if it were to be included as an illustration of an openness toward Gentiles, it is a quite minor note in an overwhelmingly Jewish symphony. Perhaps we can read the mention of Joseph of Arimathea and of the Sanhedrin as indicating that at least some of the community possessed a level of affluence enabling them to move in that circle. The reference to the "women" who followed Jesus from Galilee to Jerusalem also suggests a measure of affluence and independence for them.

Beyond these broadly sketched strokes the community reflected by the Markan passion account remains indistinct. It is, like the community behind the narrative version of Q, intensely concentrating on how one ought to live righteously before God. *This* Jewish-Christian community has its eyes on its present responsibility of giving itself over to God's will and is not focused on a future, apocalyptic triumphing of the elect.

Chapter Four

Assimilation and a Focus on Discipleship

The distinctive features of Mark's narrative line reflecting the characteristics of the Q material (QN) and of the narrative line emphasizing the obedience unto death of the Son of Man (Passion Narrative = PN) identify them as, at one time, discrete stages of the composition of our present text of Mark. Another stage occurred when they were assimilated to each other with the minimal modifications that such joining required; most significant of these changes was the joining of the titles "Christ" (the emphasis of the PN) and "Son of God" (the emphasis of QN) in 1:1; 14:61–62; and 15:39. The interest in moving *from* the focus on *the events of Jesus' life,* his authoritative teaching and his death, *to paradigms of discipleship* for the period *after* Jesus indicates yet another stage of the developing text of Mark; the effect of the motif of Jesus' privately explaining the secrets of the kingdom of God to his disciples (4:10–20) and of his private disclosures to his disciples about his impending death and resurrection (8:31; 9:31; 10:33–34) create a sense of a secrecy; indeed, when 10:46–52 is bracketed with 8:22–26, the resulting text (8:22–10:52) becomes focused on the "secret" of the correct understanding, not of the kingdom of God, but of the death and resurrection of Jesus. As described below, the modifications made to QN and PN bring into being for the first time the "Gospel" of Mark, a text nearly identical to, but not yet the same as, our present text.

Putting Mark's Gospel Together

If for now we leave aside the numerous explanatory phrasings that occur passim and imply an established text,[1] it is possible for us to recognize

---

1. In chapter 5 I review these phrasings in detail; they are evidence for a yet later phase in the composition history Mark's Gospel as we now have it. The explanatory phrasings amend

that the remaining portions of the present text of Mark's Gospel have two interests: (1) the accommodation of the narrative version of Q to the passion account, emphasizing Jesus' radical obedience to the Father (the "Son of Adam" Christology of Paul); and (2) an emphasis on discipleship as a pursuit of something "secret" and "hidden" in Jesus' teaching. Let us begin at the beginning.

Mark 1:1

"The beginning of the 'Good News!' about Jesus CHRIST, a SON OF GOD...." This phrasing provides a "title" to the entire new work. It brings together into alignment the three identifying names: Jesus, Christ, Son of God. The title "Christ" is forever linked with the account of Jesus' death, even though it does not express the theological interests of that account; and the title "Son of God" is a condensed symbol for the figure of Q's narrative version, in view of the baptism account, the transfiguration account, and the demonic recognitions of Jesus' identity. Here the text links both of these titles to the story of Jesus, whose death and resurrection were the "good news" early Christianity proclaimed. By placing 1:1 before the narrative version of Q, Mark has both anticipated the passion account and subordinated the "Christ" interpretation of Jesus to the "Son of God" interpretation.

By recognizing the fragmentary nature of 1:1 as a "title" one eliminates the awkwardness of Mark's text. The first full sentence of the Gospel is, therefore, the comparison "Just as it was written...," "there was John..." (1:2, 4).

Mark 2:13–3:6

The material of the narrative version of Q has, through 2:12, emphasized that the Spirit of God was with Jesus, enabling him to teach and to heal and to cast out demons. His appearance among men has led to "everyone" being "astonished and glorifying God" (2:12). Mark continues in 3:7 with an "enormous crowd" following him; the summary verses in 3:10–12 reiterate the themes of the material up to 2:12.

But Mark places between 2:12 and 3:7 a quite different narrative line. Mark introduces the Pharisees as opponents to Jesus and narrates three

---

a text for clarity to a larger audience, one presumed to be unfamiliar with the Jewish customs and terms embedded in that text. The text amended by these explanatory phrasings would have been QN plus PN, as assimilated by the changes described in this chapter, the penultimate version of Mark's Gospel, before the present text we have today.

controversies, two of them focused upon Jesus' different sense of the Sabbath observance. All this leads to the concluding comment by the narrator that "the Pharisees went away and immediately formed a plan with the Herodians against him in order that they might destroy him" (3:6). As is widely recognized, this is the evangelist's first intimation that the story of the Son of God might not end in the triumphant realization of the kingdom of God but in something quite different. It echoes the preoccupation of the opponents of Jesus in the passion account and also the plan of the unrighteous in the Wisdom of Solomon:

> [17]Let us see if his words are true, and let us test what will happen at the end of his life; [18]for if the righteous man is God's son, he will help him, and will deliver him from the hand of his adversaries. [19]Let us test him with insult and torture, that we may find out how gentle he is, and make trial of his forbearance. [20]Let us condemn him to a shameful death, for, according to what he says, he will be protected. (Wis 2:17-20 RSV)

There are two clear indications that this material in Mark 2:13-3:6 is an intrusion into the narrative version of the Q material. It opens with a scene introducing the first controversy over Jesus' eating with tax collectors and sinners, a scene that artificially patterns the call of Levi after the call of the first disciples in 1:16-20. Moreover, following it is an extensive summary of general circumstances in 3:7-12, which serves to restore the reader to the plot line of the narrative version of Q.

The insertion of 2:13-3:6 thus anticipates the passion account, although it does not focus on discipleship.

Mark 3:14a, 16-20

It is at the end of these verses that their character as an insertion becomes apparent. The scene in 3:20 is of Jesus in a house, with so dense a crowd that it is not possible even to eat "bread," a comment that betrays a knowledge already of the themes of 6:30 through 8:21. But even more telling is that discontinuity between 3:20 and 3:21: after 3:20 situates Jesus in a house, 3:21 has those close to him going *out* to restrain him. That image of others going *out* to Jesus follows quite straightforwardly from the setting expressed in QN 3:13, "And he went up into the hills," where he gives "those whom he wanted" the "authority to expel demons" (3:15). The reaction in QN 3:21-22 is precisely over the matter of casting out demons. Indeed, if one were to omit 3:14, 16-20 from the narrative, there would be no sense of something missing. With those verses present, there instead is a sense of a narrative interruption, a disruption of focus that is awkward and unnecessary.

The insertion of 3:14a, 16–20 thus provides a focus on the authoritative disciples in the story of Jesus; they are the Twelve, including "Judas Iscariot, who also betrayed him" (3:19), thus anticipating again the passion account in the midst of the narrative version of Q.

Mark 4:10–20, 34

Here Mark modifies the eschatological character of the parable chapter of Q's narrative version to focus on discipleship and the challenges to discipleship.

The eschatological thrust of the parable collection is clear from the challenges in 4:9 and 23: Let the one who has hearing, hear! But it is absolutely evident in the image of everything being made manifest (4:21–22), of a measured response being given to one's actions (4:24), of what one has being taken away (4:25), of a harvest (4:26–29). In that context, the parable of the Sower becomes a *challenge* to do the will of God (3:24); this was the climactic ending to the scene that began in 3:21, and the parable addresses the challenge of doing the will of God in the last days before the kingdom of God is established (4:30–32).

The insertions in 4:10–20, 34 change the setting from Jesus in a boat, teaching the crowd on the shore, to Jesus alone with those around him who again include "the Twelve"(!). But far more startling is the change of focus. The eschatological recedes and is replaced by an emphasis upon response to "the word" in an ongoing world; there will be "oppression or persecution" (4:17) and "worries of the age" (4:19), including "the deception of wealth and the craving for other things." This is a description of different kinds of discipleship, from the initially enthusiastic but shallow, through to the deeply rooted and fruit-bearing. Here the awareness of the difficulty of sustaining discipleship as the concerns of the present press in upon the disciple has replaced the immediacy of the end-time.

Different also is the portrayal of Jesus' ministry. Until 4:10, Jesus' mission has been to go from town to town, preaching to everyone (1:38). There has been an element of secrecy in the narrative line before this, but it has been focused on the correct understanding of Jesus as the Son of God; while the reader/hearer of Mark's account has been aware of Jesus' relationship to the Father, the general public has not, and the demonic world must be silenced to preserve that situation. Now Jesus is seen as speaking of "the secret of the kingdom of God" (4:11); what the content of that "secret" is remains unstated, but Jesus is shown as "explaining" everything to the disciples (4:34). Yet the inconsistency of this material (4:10–20, 34) with the context into which it has been inserted is apparent; the very disciples to whom Jesus had "explained everything" have "no faith" (4:40) in the very next scene and in subsequent scenes.

Mark 4:34 is also an editorial change to pick up the altered view of the disciples accomplished by the insertion of 4:11.

Mark 6:14–29

Here Mark most awkwardly places the tradition concerning the death of John the Baptist. The narrative line has Jesus traveling around the villages (6:6) and calling "the Twelve" to himself (6:7) in order to commission them (6:8–11); they then go out and preach and cast out many demons and heal many sick persons (6:12–13). Mark links the tradition about the Baptist into this sequence with the phrasing that King Herod Antipas has heard about all this because his (presumably Jesus') name has become well-known, and Herod thinks he is the Baptist raised from the dead. The text thus changes the focus from Jesus' commissioning disciples to continue his work and puts it on telling about the end of the Baptist's life. Mark continues the narrative line seamlessly, however, in 6:30, where the "apostles" come back to Jesus to report everything that they have done; indeed, a reader would never miss 6:14–29 if the redactor had omitted it from the sequence of 6:6–13, 30. One can also argue that 6:30–8:21 is a coherent whole, both structurally and thematically, employing throughout a metaphor on "bread."[2] Nothing in 6:14–29 anchors that material to the materials preceding it or following it, except the awkward comment in 6:14 attributing Jesus' powers to the risen Baptist's presence in him.

Yet, as many have observed, this material does anticipate the death of Jesus and does raise the perspective of resurrection (6:14). It thus, like 3:6, prepares the reader for the eventual outcome of Jesus' story. Scholars have recognized the motif of foreshadowing events as an element of the Markan Gospel.[3] I suggest that the phenomenon of the foreshadowing

---

2. See Hugh Humphrey, "Jesus as Wisdom in Mark," *Biblical Theology Bulletin* 19 (1989): QN 84, and *"He Is Risen!" A New Reading of Mark's Gospel* (New York: Paulist Press, 1992), 56–74, esp. 57.

3. Frank J. Moloney thus writes, "One [narrative unit] flows into the other, looks back to issues already mentioned, and hints at themes yet to come"; cf. Moloney, *The Gospel of Mark:*

of events in the present text of Mark's Gospel comes about precisely because the redactor has inserted later materials into earlier texts, which in turn create the foreshadowing.

Mark 6:14–29 is obviously not focused on Jesus, though all of the rest of the materials before 6:14 and after 6:29 are so focused. This is a tradition about the death of the Baptist that is strikingly anomalous in the story about Jesus bringing the gospel of God's kingdom to the people of Israel. Like other insertions made when this Gospel fused the narrative version of Q and the passion account, however, the story both prepares for the passion account and provides a commentary on discipleship. The Baptist, like Jesus, was a holy and righteous man (6:20), and unwilling to compromise God's will for political and personal expedience; for that, he was put to death. Both the Baptist then and Jesus later provide models of giving all that one has, even to the point of death, in submission to the will of God. Thus, the text expresses the theology of the passion account amid Q's narrative version and presents a lesson on discipleship — all in the context of Jesus' commissioning of the Twelve (6:6–13).

Mark 8:27–33

There are a number of reasons to believe that 8:27–33 is an insertion reflecting the perspectives of the passion account into the narrative version of Q. First, in 8:31 it offers a synopsis of the PN, thereby betraying knowledge of it. Second, it introduces the reader to the Son of Man, not in the eschatological sense of 2:10 and 8:38 (its immediately following context) or 13:26, but as a reference to the suffering and dying Jesus, who will be raised from the dead. The text thus replaces the eschatological perspective that has dominated Mark's account until now, and continues to be emphasized in the immediately following section (8:34–9:1), and focuses on the present and the threat to Jesus' life first voiced by the insertion of 2:13–3:6. Third, it somewhat artlessly introduces this insertion with the same formula as the last insertion (6:14–29), a series of identifications about whom Jesus was thought to be: first, the Baptist; then, Elijah; then, one of the prophets. Fourth, the purpose of the recitation of identifications becomes clear with Peter's acclamation of Jesus as "the Christ," the *false* title under which Jesus will be put to death in

---

A Commentary (Peabody, MA: Hendrickson, 2002), 19. See also Joanna Dewey, "Mark as Interwoven Tapestry: Forecasts and Echoes for a Listening Audience," *Catholic Biblical Quarterly* 53, no. 2 (1991): 221–36; and Elizabeth Struthers Malbon, "Echoes and Foreshadowings in Mark 4–8: Reading and Rereading," *Journal of Biblical Literature* 112, no. 2 (1993): 211–30.

the passion account; notice that Jesus warns against the use of that title. Fifth, Peter is here the one who illustrates weak and misunderstanding discipleship, just as he will in the material inserted into the passion account at 14:29–31, and 14:54, 66–72. Finally, this passage at its climax, embodied in the rebuke to Peter, states that Jesus' emptying of himself to the will of God,[4] which is the theology of the passion account, is being committed to the things of God (8:33).

The purpose of this insertion is clear. At this point the narrative version of Q has presented Jesus' teaching about saving one's life in the sense of being ready when the Son of Man (eschatological sense) comes in the glory of his Father with the holy angels (8:38); Jesus has spoken of a person having to "take his cross and follow me" (8:34). What this insertion does is focus attention on the paradox of 8:35: "For whoever wants to save his life, will destroy it; but whoever destroys his life will save it." And the insertion of 8:27–33 focuses attention on the deeper, secret meaning of that paradox by imposing upon the narrative version of Q, together with the subsequent passion predictions in 9:31 and 10:33–34 and other alterations, a coherent and unified structure. Others have recognized that 8:27–10:45 is a coherent whole;[5] some would say that the twin healing of blind men in 8:22–26 and 10:46–52 are framing passages for this section.[6] Some would say that the result is to create a central, pivotal section for the entire Gospel. In any event, the insertion creates the interpretative focus for the material that follows up to 10:45.[7]

Here I advance a hypothesis about the so-called "Secret Gospel of Mark."[8] We have been tracing a composition history for the Gospel

---

4. Implicit in Jesus' statement that the Son of Man must suffer (8:31).

5. E. R. Kalin, " 'That I May See': Christology and Ecclesiology in Mark," *Currents in Theology and Mission* 20, no. 6 (1993): 445–54.

6. Cf., e.g., Ernest Best, "Discipleship in Mark: Mark 8.22–10.52," *Scottish Journal of Theology* 23 (1970): 323–37; and M. N. Keller, "Opening Blind Eyes: A Revisioning of Mark 8:22–10:52," *Biblical Theology Bulletin* 31, no. 4 (2001): 151–57.

7. Hugh M. Humphrey, *"He Is Risen!" A New Reading of Mark's Gospel* (New York: Paulist Press, 1992), 75–96.

8. The discussion began with the publication in 1973 of the text of the so-called "Secret Gospel of Mark" by Morton Smith: *Clement of Alexandria and a Secret Gospel of Mark* (Cambridge, MA: Harvard University Press, 1973). Cf. more recently Philip Sellew, "Secret Mark and the History of Canonical Mark," in *The Future of Christianity: Essays in Honor of Helmut Koester* (ed. Birger A. Pearson, A. Thomas Kraabel, and George W. E. Nickelsburg; Minneapolis, MN: Fortress, 1991), 242–57; and C. W. Hedrick and N. Olympiou, "Secret Mark: New Photographs, New Witnesses," *The Fourth R* [Santa Rosa, CA] 13, no. 5 (2000): 3–11, 14–16.

of Mark, one that accords with patristic testimony suggesting that several versions of Mark's Gospel existed. I propose that the QN and PN had separate existence for a time, and then the creation of another text assimilated the two and inserted 8:27–33 as the interpretative key for the eschatological sense of 8:34–9:1. This redaction created a Gospel in which human events like Jesus' death on the cross hold secret meaning concerning "the things of God" (8:33). What Jesus teaches as a paradox, that one must destroy his life in order to save it, Jesus graphically demonstrates by his own obedience unto death and God's subsequent raising of him from the dead. But this radical, ultimate selflessness is not natural; it goes against our rational sense of self-preservation and our innate selfishness. "The things of men" (8:33) are self and the extension of self in families and property and status. The resurrection of Jesus shows that the "secret" or "mystery" of God's will for humankind is that all these must be "lost" in order for one to be "saved." The very construction of 8:27–10:45 as a unified whole — through the insertion of 8:27–33 and the following insertions — creates an enormously more profound text, a statement in narrative form of the secret will of God for men and women. We can appropriately call it a "secret Gospel," not in the sense that its existence is to be kept secret, but in the sense that it expresses the depth of the meaning of Jesus' death and of God's will.

Clement of Alexandria might well have wanted to restrict access to this longer and more complex text, this "secret Gospel." That may have had more to do with the stages of introduction of converts to the depth of Christian discipleship than to any effort to hide the longer text as esoteric and mysterious. Paul himself observes that some early converts are still "babes" (1 Cor 3:1–2), so that he cannot feed them the "wisdom" that he teaches to the spiritually mature (2:6). The separate accounts of Jesus as the eschatological prophet filled with the Wisdom of God, and of Jesus as the righteous one falsely accused and sentenced to death, only to be raised by God from the dead — these were basic elements for instructing new converts to Christianity. But the necessity of a complete giving of self, even unto death, requires an understanding of discipleship built upon the rock of deep spirituality. The church in history and even today provides evidence of how difficult it has been for believers to perceive this mysterious, secret wisdom of "the things of God." Even today people give allegiance to the miracle-working prophetic figure and to the risen Jesus without understanding the personal, ethical commitment of true discipleship to Jesus and, hence, what obedience to the will of God requires. In this one quite real sense, the present text of the Gospel of Mark is, indeed, *still* a "secret" Gospel.

Mark 9:9–13

The insertion of 9:9–13 into QN — which has just presented the transfiguration of Jesus (9:2–8) and disclosed to Peter, James, and John what the baptism account had disclosed to Jesus, that Jesus was God's beloved Son — alters the direction of the narrative. The voice from the cloud directly commands these disciples to "Listen to him!" and the context in which Moses appears and then disappears from view makes the instruction clear: Listen to Jesus' interpretation of Moses and his law. Now Jesus instructs them not to speak of the transfiguration event "until the Son of Man had risen from the dead" (9:9), thus effectively anticipating yet again the passion account. The insertion serves the function also of a mini-commentary on the narrative version of Q's allusion to Elijah (9:4–5) and the tradition that he had to come before the end-time could occur (Mal 4:5). Jesus' response that "Elijah has come, and they did to him whatever they wanted, just as it is written concerning him" (9:13) can only be a reference to the Baptist, as Matthew also clearly understands (Matt 17:13). The phrasing "just as it is written concerning him" (Mark 9:13) is particularly interesting; the same hand that made the insertion of 6:14–29 seems to be responsible for this insertion.

Mark 9:30–32

This second prediction of the passion, death, and resurrection of the Son of Man intrudes upon the materials around it. The preceding passage spoke of the inability of the disciples to cast out a dumb spirit and the necessity of faith (9:14–29). The following passage, against an eschatological context (9:39–50), expresses yet again the fundamental paradox, found in 8:34, of living selflessly in order to save oneself: "If anyone wants to be first, let him be last of all and servant of everyone" (9:35). Mark 9:30–32, by contrast, brings the reader forward to the death of this miracle-working prophet of the end-time. The phrasing that introduces the setting for the passion prediction is so general that the prediction could have been located anywhere and need not have appeared here. The subsequent reference to Capharnaum (9:33) may depend upon this setting in 9:30 since the setting in 9:28 was a "house," matching the setting in 9:33 for Jesus and the disciples.

More striking is the fact that in the immediately preceding scene, in 9:28–29, the disciples had no hesitation in asking Jesus why they had been unable to cast out the dumb spirit, yet in 9:30–32 after Jesus' prediction of his passion and death the disciples, not understanding the saying, are "afraid" to ask him. In the space of five verses, the disciples have moved from being unafraid to ask questions to being afraid to ask him about the passion prediction!

Finally, if it is correct that 8:27–10:45 is the central section of Mark's present text,[9] then this passage would be the central passion prediction, framed by episodes in which Jesus interacts with his disciples. Two elements of this brief passage support the contention made here that this expansion of the narrative version of Q and of the earlier passion account created a "secret" Gospel, a Gospel in which the wisdom of God for humankind's righteousness was a hidden and secret wisdom, unimaginable to human reason. Jesus is seen "teaching" his disciples (9:31) but does not want anyone else to know what he is teaching (9:30); the brief comment in 9:32 that the disciples "did not understand the saying, and they were afraid to ask him" expresses a quite human reaction. If God's will is that one must give selflessly to others, even to the point of death, that is the exact opposite of our human "wisdom,"[10] in which we strive to extend ourselves by acquisition of persons and things. The reaction of the disciples is the reaction of all: we don't want to understand.

Although 9:30–32 is but three verses long, its position and its content make it an apt expression of the central theme of Mark's present text: in Jesus' acceptance of the Father's will for him that he die and triumph over death, all who are disciples have a revelation of how we too must live, losing oneself (8:34), being last of all (9:35). The kenotic emphasis of the passion account has, therefore, intruded upon and here qualified the eschatological emphases of the materials that surround this insertion.

Mark 10:32–34, 35–45

The redactor completed the enterprise of creating the unified block of materials we now find in 8:27–10:45 by inserting two long passages, 10:32–34 and 10:35–45. As in the case of inserting the two previous

---

9. Cf. Humphrey, "*He Is Risen!*" 75–96. The theme of this central section of Mark is "The Secret Wisdom and True Response to God: Giving All, to All, Gains All."

10. Again, the agreement with the perspectives of Paul's First Letter to the Corinthians is clear. Cf. 1 Cor 1:21–30.

passion predictions, the insertion of these two passages stands in tension with the narrative line that precedes them. Jesus has been speaking of the kingdom of God (10:23), which is eschatological; the disciples understand that Jesus is speaking about being "saved" (10:26), and Jesus makes it clear that he is talking about "eternal life in the age to come" (10:30). In that immediate context the paradox of 8:34 has the sound of a threat of judgment: "Many who are first...will be last, and the last, first" (10:31). That saying has the ring of a climax, similar to the saying in 4:9: "Whoever has ears to hear, let him hear!"

The two insertions that begin at 10:32, however, are focused both on the impending death of Jesus and on discipleship.

Mark 10:32–34 presents yet another passion prediction, a third to form a frame with 8:31 for the materials within them, centered by the passion prediction in 9:31. The setting in this third prediction is more elaborate; the picture is of Jesus going in front of the disciples to Jerusalem, "and they were amazed, yet those who were following were afraid." The disciples seem to begin to understand what the passion predictions have been pointing toward; their amazement signals their radical failure to understand Jesus' voluntarily going toward his death. And Jesus provides details of the events of the passion account.

Mark 10:35–45 mimics the misunderstanding of the disciples that followed the second passion prediction. When James and John seek to have a share in Jesus' personal glory at the resurrection promised at the end of each of the passion predictions, however, the passage has moved away from the promises made to any and all disciples of eternal life in the age to come (10:29–31) to the core essence of discipleship. These verses are almost a commentary on those earlier promises in 10:29–31. They had promised that *anyone* who had left everything and followed Jesus would have eternal life in the age to come. Here Jesus says that it is not given to him to decide who will participate in his glory: "It is for those for whom it has been prepared" (10:40). And the triumphant expectations of 10:31, "Many who are first...will be last, and the last, first," are explained: "Whoever among you wants to be first, shall be the slave of everyone" (10:44). The "among you" phrasing places the emphasis squarely on discipleship that is worked out as service of others within the Christian community. And the text gives the example of Jesus' own giving of self over to service, even unto death, as the paradigm of discipleship (10:45).

The beginnings of these two passages specifically identify Jesus, and the reader understands that the references to "the Son Man" in 10:33 and 10:45 are to him. So also, the reference to Jesus as "Teacher" in 10:35 brings that title for the eschatological prophet of the narrative version of Q into alignment with the Son of Man figure in the passion account. The eschatological, future sense of Son of Man has sharply receded as the narrative approaches the passion account.

And a final comment concerning 10:35–45: In the concentric structure that the redactor has imposed upon these materials by inserting the three passion predictions,[11] we can see this material in 10:35–45 as corresponding in turn to 8:27–30. In both of these passages, the text has Jesus alone with his disciples, narrates a dialogue, and corrects a misunderstanding.

Mark 10:46–52

The construction of the central section of Mark's Gospel, resulting from the insertion of 8:27–33 and subsequent changes through to 10:45, appears immediately after a healing of a blind man in 8:22–26. To provide a frame for the central section, another healing of a blind man is inserted here at 10:46–52. The two healings are markedly different. In the first one, the healing does not immediately happen, presumably because the blind man does not initially have an adequate faith. In this second healing, Bartimaeus has the exemplary faith of a disciple.

Bartimaeus calls out to Jesus as "Son of David," anticipating the messianic overtones of Jesus' entry into Jerusalem and also the intensification of that title in the passion account into the charge of being the Messiah. This passage, however, is focused much more on the matter of being a disciple who correctly "sees" what Jesus has been teaching as the secret wisdom of God. Just as all men are "blind," humanly speaking, to what God really requires of them, so also is Bartimaeus. Just as he cries out, "Master, that I might see!" (10:51), so also must every disciple daily cry out in faith. That very crying out is the faith that accepts the dominion of God's will over all, a faith that "has saved you" (10:52). And so Bartimaeus — like all who cry out for the removal of their human and natural antipathy to this giving of self, for sight and not blindness — is enabled to see and "followed him *on the way*" (10:52). "On the way" in these

---

11. Thus Humphrey, *"He Is Risen!"* 79.

contexts is the way of discipleship, and the phrase appears concentrated in this central part of Mark's Gospel: 8:27; 9:33, 34; 10:32; 10:52.

This healing story, therefore, provides a consolation to the reader. Although the disciples of Jesus' immediate company can be so blind as not to understand what he is saying (8:18) and the teaching of the passion predictions, which he spoke "openly" to them (8:32), Bartimaeus illustrates a disciple's faith giving him the sight that can enable true discipleship and following of Jesus "on the way" to the complete giving of self to others.

The perspectives of the narrative version of Q have receded since 10:31 and its ominous climax.

Mark 11:1–10, 11b–15a, 18–27

The narrative version of Q appears to have ended with a confrontation over Jesus' authority in the very heart of Jerusalem. His putting a lower value on the religiosity of sacrifice and burnt offerings is symbolized by his cleansing of the temple (11:15b–17) and confirmed by his approval of the scribe's statement of the priority of love of God and neighbor over all other practices (12:33). Yet that very challenge to the foundations of the Jewish religion then brings out counterchallenges to his authority and Jesus' final eschatological discourse, in chapter 13. Mark has to refocus this material in order to make it prepare for the passion account, beginning in chapter 14 of our present text.

Two features of 11:1–10 distinguish it. The passage begins with Jesus giving a lengthy instruction to the disciples to go into the village and describing what will happen as they follow out his instructions. The text places an emphasis on everything unfolding just as Jesus has said it will. In comparing this with the beginning of the passion account, one finds a quite similar pattern, ending in 14:16 by saying, "The disciples... found it just as he had told them," a phrasing that echoes 11:6: "just as Jesus had said." In addition to this parallel of form with the introduction to the passion account, there is the clear interest in placing a messianic interpretation of Jesus' entrance into Jerusalem. Added to the citation of Ps 118:26 is the phrasing "Blessed is the coming kingdom of our father David!" That citation recalls the cry of Bartimaeus in the material inserted in 10:46–52; it also anticipates the charge against Jesus that he is "the King of the Jews" in the passion account (esp. 14:61–62; 15:2–15:26). The effect of 11:1–10, therefore, is to mute the eschatological emphasis of the narrative account of Q and to redirect attention to a messianic interpretation of Jesus that is tightly associated with the account of his death. As in 14:12–16, Jesus knows what events will unfold and accepts them, demonstrating again the acceptance of the Father's will for him that is characteristic of the passion account's emphasis on Jesus' obedience.

Yet another observation about 11:1–10: The description reports a quite public and large-scale event that remains strangely unmentioned in any subsequent scene in the Gospel. Jesus enters the temple to look around like a tourist, retreats to Bethany, returns the next day to cleanse the temple, then goes back to sleep in Bethany. When he returns to Jerusalem and the temple on the third day, religious leaders question his "authority," but they make no comment about the messianic recognition accorded to him as he entered Jerusalem two days earlier. The absence of comment upon the scene narrated in 11:1–10 supports the view that it is an insertion into existing narrative lines.

The two passages recounting the unfortunate fig tree encountered between Bethany and Jerusalem also appear to be insertions into the narrative account of Q. They frame and interpret the cleansing of the temple scene in 11:15b–17.

Mark 12:1–12

In the narrative version of Q the open challenge to Jesus' "authority" that begins in 11:27b[12] expands into a number of questions from various religious groups, ending with the observation in 12:34 that "no one anymore dared to question him." These challenges are notable for their focus upon the Jewish scriptural tradition. The text presents Jesus as knowing the Scripture better than his religious opponents (who are "very wrong" [12:27]) and citing it extensively. The redactor has inserted the parable in 12:1–12 into this extended narrative about Jesus' authority to correctly interpret the will of God expressed in the Jewish Scriptures. The parable is a commentary on the entire section of controversies that surrounds it. It concerns the vineyard (Israel) with a hedge around it (the law of Moses), which a man (God) plants and then gives over to others (the religious leaders of the Jews). When it is time for the vineyard to bear fruit (righteousness), the man sends servants (prophets) to the farmers, who mistreat the servants. He sends his son/heir (Jesus), and the farmers kill him and throw him out of the vineyard (12:8). So the man

---

12. In Mk 2:5–12, the questioning of the scribes is among themselves and private.

wreaks vengeance on the farmers and "will give the vineyard to others" (Gentiles/Christians). The citation of the rejected stone becoming the cornerstone anticipates the reversal of the fate of Jesus (resurrection).

The parable anticipates the death of the Son/Heir, who clearly is Jesus, and thus conflicts with QN's focus. In the narrative version of Q, Jesus is the eschatological prophet of God's Wisdom, announcing the coming judgment by the Son of Man and doing so with "authority." The parable's purpose is solely to prepare for the passion account.

Mark 12:35–37

After the closing remark at the end of 12:34, the text pictures Jesus as responding (to the whole preceding set of controversies?) with a question of his own: "How can the scribes say: 'The Christ is the Son of David'?" Here Mark explicitly links the Messiah title of the passion account with two earlier insertions, the "Son of David" acclamations of Bartimaeus and of the crowd when Jesus entered Jerusalem. Yet the purpose of the question is to challenge the equation! If the Messiah is the son of David, whose role as Messiah is to restore the kingdom of David, then David would be superior to him both as father and as paradigm. Yet, since David the psalmist speaks of "my lord," the Messiah must be something quite more than just David's son. Jesus, who will be put to death as "the King of the Jews," the "Christ," will be shown by his resurrection to be far more than just a descendant of David inaugurating "the kingdom of our father David" (11:10). In its present context, however, readers cannot completely understand this saying because the text has not yet narrated the passion of Jesus. As part of the assimilated traditions, in the text that results from joining the QN with the PN, this saying again suggests the element of a secret not publicly known (no one gives an answer to the dilemma posed by Jesus) that concerns the identity of Jesus.

Mark 12:41–44

Mark sets this short scene apart from the preceding scenes by its more specific location (Jesus is in the temple in 11:27 [and 12:35], then comes out of the temple in 13:1, but in 12:41 he is across from the treasury). The text also distinguishes this account by letting it illustrate how one ought to live. With approval Jesus points out the widow's contributing two small copper coins and makes her an example for giving "everything she had, her whole existence!" (12:44). The earlier episode of the

Baptist's death interrupted the flow of the narrative to illustrate a righteousness to the point of death; likewise, this anecdote interrupts the narrative flow[13] to illustrate the same point, the emptying of self that characterizes the passion account. Here the story of Jesus is not so much in focus as the lesson provided for discipleship.

The Second-Person Elements in Chapter 13

The narrative account of the Q material ended as Q did, with an eschatological discourse that spoke directly and warningly about the judgment the Son of Man would bring. Much of chapter 13 speaks directly to the question of Peter, James, and John about the sign that all these things are about to be accomplished. Two kinds of material appear in chapter 13, however, and one can easily distinguish them by their syntax: materials in the form of direct address, and those in the third person. The third-person sayings are sharply eschatological; the direct-address ones tone down those eschatological expectations. The third-person discourse focuses on provisions for "the elect," and yet the direct address urges caution: "Take care..." occurs in 13:5, 9, 23, 33; cf. 35, 37. When one separates the second-person comments from the third-person eschatological materials, their nature as amendments easing the harshness of that end-time picture is clear.

Mark 14:3–9

Since the passion account begins at 14:1, insertions made after that point have as their focus some continuing presentation of Jesus from the narrative version of Q. This passage also employs the motif of a residence in Bethany, where Jesus is a guest, adding the detail that it was "the house of Simon the leper" (14:3). With its reference to "the good news" being preached (14:9), it picks up a theme from earlier materials where both Jesus and the disciples are preaching the gospel of the kingdom of God. So, too, the compassion for the poor in 14:5–7 recalls the compassion for the hungry in 8:2.

This passage anticipates the death of Jesus with Jesus' remark in 14:8 that "she anointed my body in anticipation of its burial," but its primary purpose is to present a model of discipleship. In that respect it is quite like the insertion of the materials about the Baptist's death (6:14–29)

---

13. It could be omitted and the narrative line would flow easily from Mark 12:40 to 13:1. In fact, the connection between the "judgment" of 12:40 and the eschatological thrust of 13:2ff. would be even stronger.

and about the widow giving all she had, her whole existence (12:41–44). Here Jesus praises the anointing woman: "What she was able to do, she did" (14:8). Just as Jesus presents the widow to the disciples as a model (12:44), so also for the woman here: "Wherever the 'good news!' is preached through the world, what this woman has done will also be spoken of in memory of her" (14:9). That phrasing also speaks of a period after Jesus' ministry and death. It is a time frame that has not otherwise been in focus except for the second-person cautions of chapter 13, an extended time of discipleship well beyond the time of Jesus.

Mark 14:28, 29–31

The scene in 14:26–27 has moved Jesus to the Mount of Olives for his announcement that all the disciples will be scandalized by his betrayal and arrest and death, which will shortly be unfolding; the "shepherd" will be struck and the "sheep" scattered (Zech 13:7). The reference in 14:28 to Jesus' "being raised up" provides the same note of triumph over death as did the climactic statements of the passion predictions in 8:31; 9:31; 10:33–34. With the case of the last insertion in 14:3–9, this one moves the focus forward to a time beyond Jesus' death and resurrection and provides the basis for the later announcement of the young man at the tomb, in 16:7. This single verse (14:28) anticipates the period of early Christian discipleship to follow Jesus' death and resurrection. Everything leading up to that period is but "the beginning," as Mark announces in 1:1.

The matter of discipleship is even more in focus in 14:29–31, with Peter's promise of faithful discipleship and Jesus' rebuke, foretelling Peter's betrayal; the similarity of form with 8:32–33 suggests that the hand responsible for the insertion there is responsible for this one. In 8:32–33 Peter's response betrayed a failure to understand the things of God because he was thinking in human terms; so here also in 14:29–31 Peter makes a humanly understandable vow of friendship, which Jesus knows will shortly yield to the pressure of events; Peter is still thinking in human terms.

The material in 14:29–31 presents a *negative* model of discipleship to balance the examples of the Baptist, the widow, and the anointing woman. In the explanation of the parable of the Sower, Mark already anticipated the tragedy of discipleship that fails: the "seed" sown on the rocky ground are disciples who because of oppression or persecution "fall away" (4:16–17). Peter will become *the* negative model of discipleship before this chapter ends; as Jesus here predicts, he denies Jesus three times before the cock crows thrice.

Mark 14:54, 66–72

The narrative marks the trial of Jesus before the high priest as a whole by references to Jesus' being "led away," first to the high priest in 14:53, and then after that trial, to Pilate (15:1). The materials within 14:53–15:1 that mention Peter, however, have no such anchor. If the text omitted 14:54 and 14:66–72, readers would never miss these verses because the narrative line does not require them. They have as their only purpose the completion of the picture of negative discipleship begun in 14:29–31. Yet there is a glimpse of hope offered in the portrayal of Peter in 14:72. After three times denying the one whom he has promised never to deny, Peter "threw himself down and wept" (14:72). When thinking in human terms exhausts a person facing the mystery of God's plan and one's own failure to understand it and be obedient to it, perhaps one can only weep as Peter did. The angel at the tomb will commission the women to tell the disciples about the risen Jesus and, oh yes, include Peter too. Peter's weeping demonstrates a remorse that is accepted. The negative model of discipleship is rescued by that simple act of Peter throwing himself down and weeping at his weakness; it thus presents a positive sign for others who, like Peter, are the seed sown on rocky ground.[14]

Mark 15:38–39

It is apparent that these two verses change the focus of what precedes and follows them, where the focus is on the story of Jesus' death and burial. The two comments made here are a narrator's commentary on the significance of Jesus' death as perceived from both a Jewish and a non-Jewish point of view. These two verses stand as a commentary on Jesus' beginning of the recitation of Ps 22 in Mark 15:34 and on Jesus' death in 15:37. They combine the interests of the narrative version of Q and earlier insertions identified above.

On the one hand, the observation that "the inner curtain of the temple was torn in two from top to bottom" provides a response to the challenges made to Jesus in the temple in 11:27–34 (= QN) and the insertion

---

14. Is it only coincidence that Matthew has Jesus say in Matt 16:18, "You are Peter, and on this rock I will build my church" (NRSV).

into that material of the parable of the vineyard, particularly of Jesus' ominous words in 12:9 that "he [God] will give the vineyard [Israel] to others." They also provide an announcement that the eschatological program Jesus announced in chapter 13 (= QN) has begun; the stone building may still stand now (13:2), but the heart and soul of the building and of the Jewish people have been violated; its curtained mystery is gone. Finally, this is the narrator's response to the charge made against Jesus in 14:58 and remembered in 15:29, that he would "pull down the temple made by hands and in three days, ... build another not made by hands." The rending of the temple veil at Jesus' death was the beginning of that.

On the other hand, the centurion's comment is an immediate reaction to Jesus' giving up the spirit in 15:37. The same verb ($\dot{\epsilon}\xi\dot{\epsilon}\pi\nu\epsilon\nu\sigma\epsilon\nu$ is used in 15:39, but preceded by the adverbial comment "in this way," which places an emphasis on the manner by which Jesus "breathed his last" and died; it underscores Jesus' death as being an ideal, paradigmatic model for all. Just as the Baptist's death in 6:14–29 and the widow's gift of her "whole existence" in 12:41–44 were insertions to illustrate the fundamental nature of discipleship in anticipation of Jesus' death, so now Mark unmistakably points out Jesus' death as *the model* for discipleship by the simple little adverbial comment: "in this way." Even if one cannot expect that a Roman centurion could know the content of Ps 22, with its ringing acceptance of the dominion of God and its assurance that "all the ends of the earth ... shall turn to the LORD" (Ps 22:27 NRSV), the text here presents him as though he does know the psalm. His admiration of Jesus as "truly" being "a Son of God" reiterates both the kenotic theology of the hymn in Phil 2 and of the passion account, and also the favored title for Jesus in the narrative version of Q. As a consequence, this insertion provides the often-noticed "bracket" with the opening scene of Jesus' baptism, in which the voice from heaven calls him God's beloved "Son" and the Spirit comes down upon him (1:10–11 = QN).

The Community Reflected by These Additions to the Text of Mark

The joining of the narrative version of Q and the passion account was not a case of the former being simply placed as "a long introduction" to the latter. Although both narrative lines centered on Jesus, the theological appraisal of him was significantly different in each. The QN portrays Jesus as the prophetic figure, filled with the authority of God's Spirit and announcing the eschatological Son of Man and the kingdom of God. Thus, if the redactor had placed the QN before the PN without adjustments, it could not easily have introduced the PN and its portrayal of a Son of Man who is obedient to God's will, even to the point of suffering and dying on the cross. The intimations of that unexpected end to the story of Jesus in 2:13–3:6 and the passion predictions are perfectly understandable redactions in order to prepare the reader for Jesus' death. There is, however, the further emphasis on the implications for discipleship present in fourteen of the nineteen texts we have just reviewed, an emphasis that suggests a community for whom the newly expanded text would be enormously significant.

From the references in 4:15–19 and the second-person glosses in chapter 13, it is apparent that the keenly eschatological expectation of the narrative version of Q has receded and that the community has come to appreciate that "the end is not yet" (13:7). It is also apparent that references to "persecution" would have no relevance as a possibility not yet experienced, but would have immediate relevance in a time of persecution. In that regard, a number of the additions are all of a piece. Jesus' death was an acknowledgement of God's will for him that *he* suffer and die (8:31 and the Gethsemane scene in 14:32–42). Readers could now understand his teaching that every disciple must "take up his cross" to be enjoining a similar obedience upon anyone who would follow him (8:34). And the illustrations of the Baptist, the widow, and the woman who anointed Jesus give powerful examples of how that obedience to God's will must be a giving of everything one has, one's "complete existence" (12:44). The fact of real or impending persecution would make Jesus' complete giving of self a paradigm of discipleship for his followers.

The community for whom these additions to the earlier narratives would have relevance is thus one that has struggled with the practical hardship of following Jesus' ethical teaching while awaiting an ever more delayed eschatological day of judgment. The community would have had only its own members as social support. The ties with Judaism were broken; the temple veil had been rent apart at the death of Jesus; and the apparent openness to Gentile membership reflected by the centurion's acclamation in 15:39 would only have deepened the separation. These community members were living as Jews for whom the history and religious framework of Judaism was the lens through which to view all of life, and as Jews for whom that was being altered into a *"new covenant."* This early Christian community could only have found the alienation from family and former friends more and more difficult to sustain as the years passed and the expected return of Jesus was delayed; the "oppression" of 4:17 undoubtedly refers to suffering such social ostracism. Others of them had been committed disciples, but "the worries of the age and the deception of wealth and the craving for other things" crept in (4:19), and they left.

The members of this community who remained faithful disciples did not apparently have as consolation and support the "gifts of the Spirit" so prominent in Acts and in the Pauline churches; for Paul, the very "power" of the cross was an authenticating experience.[15] Rather, this community — responsible for the assimilation of the QN and the PN accounts through the addition of the texts identified above — was driven to a reflection upon the meaning of the death of Jesus as being a revelation of the very essence of God's will for humankind, a secret wisdom made manifest by God's approval of Jesus in the resurrection. In this respect the theology of the newly expanded Gospel replicates in narrative form the theology of Paul, especially in 1 Cor 1. Where Paul, however, would move on to illustrate the implications of this kenotic discipleship for community, Mark's community remained content to affirm for discipleship the central necessity of a complete giving of self.

In the context of a real or impending persecution, such a focus and a multiple restatement of the focus would make perfect sense. John Donahue has suggested an appropriate historical period that would correspond to these emphases;[16] "Mark's narrative world takes up the concerns of a community located in Rome which has experienced persecution, brutal executions and intrafamilial betrayal."[17] Donahue finds the association of Mark's Gospel with Rome to provide a specific context for the references to persecution in the Markan text; he accordingly believes that it was "written most likely after the turmoil that followed the death of Nero in A.D. 68, and after the Jewish war of A.D. 66–70."[18]

---

15. Cf. Paul's statements in 1 Cor 1:17 and 2:3–5.
16. John R. Donahue, "Windows and Mirrors: The Setting of Mark's Gospel," *Catholic Biblical Quarterly* 57, no. 1 (January 1995): 1–26. The texts of Mark's Gospel that Donahue uses as a basis for his view are almost entirely those we have identified as additions made when the narrative version of Q and the passion account were assimilated.
17. Ibid., 19–20.
18. Ibid., 24.

The term "persecution," however, never has such a specific reference in the ten times that it appears in the New Testament.[19] Its use reflects a range of situations, including the church in Jerusalem (Acts 8:1), persecution by Jews (13:50), persecutions (far removed from Rome) in Thessalonica (2 Thess 1:4), and Paul's personal experience of persecutions. The term seems to have a general sense rather than a specific reference.

An earlier set of circumstances provides better context. Claudius as emperor had expelled all Jews from Rome (Acts 18:2). Suetonius reports that the Jews were rioting over one "Chrestus." A Christian community of Jews at Rome, affirming its loyalty to the Christ, could in its zeal among fellow Jews have led to social upheaval in the Jewish community; as a consequence Claudius ordered all Jews, including Christian Jews, to leave Rome in 49 CE. His edict stayed in effect until his death in 54, when all Jews (and Christians) were allowed to return to Rome. Here then is another appropriate context. Both Jerome and Clement (see chap. 1, above) speak of Mark taking his "completed" Gospel to Egypt from Rome. That "completed" Gospel was the passion account PN, together with the narrative version of Q. Mark and the community he led in Egypt would have perceived themselves as "pressured" and "persecuted" (4:17) both by Jewish neighbors and Roman authorities. That social situation in turn prompted Mark's assimilation passages and the focus on "discipleship" and produced a text focused on the "secret" of the kingdom of God (4:11). In the later circumstances at Rome Donahue describes, the theology of discipleship Mark had developed would have been seen as particularly apt.

---

19. Matt 13:21; Mark 4:17; 10:30; Acts 8:1; 13:50; Rom 8:35; 2 Cor 12:10; 2 Thess 1:4; 2 Tim 3:11 (2x).

Chapter Five

The Composition History of the Gospel of Mark

Introduction: Gathering the Pieces

The evangelist whom we call Mark composed narratives to express two different early Christian theologies and then assimilated them, as we have seen. The composition process thus exposed shows that our present text of the Gospel of Mark, while the work of a single individual, is not a work written at a single sitting, in a unique context. Hence, the familiar effort in introductions and commentaries to determine a single "provenance" for Mark's Gospel is destined to fail. Instead, Mark composed his Gospel for diverse audiences and at different moments in the life of the evangelist and his communities.

Whether the narrative version of the Q material (QN) or the account of Jesus' passion and death (PN) was the earliest piece cannot be unquestionably determined; the internal evidence offered by these respective texts just does not betray an awareness of the existence of one by the other. The eschatological perspective of QN, with its sense of the imminent expectation of the judgment the Son of Man would bring, suggests an early dating; the perspective is consistent and reflects no sense of a delayed Parousia as detected in Matthew and Luke's Gospels, for example. Yet it is also difficult to believe that early Christianity would not from the very beginning have remembered the details of the death of Jesus. The account of the passion of Jesus we have traced above, however, already shows that a period of reflection has occurred: dramatic enhancements of the betrayal of Jesus and of Jesus' trials have expanded the simple kerygmatic proclamation, and the narrative of Jesus' suffering and death has been set against the backdrop of texts from the Psalms, Isaiah, Zechariah, and the Wisdom of Solomon. That phenomenon of reflection suggests for the PN, as we can recover it from the present text of Mark, a period later than that of the QN.

The testimony of the early church fathers seems to support the suggestion that Mark composed the QN material before the PN now found in the Gospel. The text nowhere explains how Mark came to be a follower of Jesus, but Clement of Alexandria remembers that Mark followed Peter for "a long time." Papias remembers that Peter had spoken ad hoc, so that Mark's account is not a complete exposition of Jesus' ministry and seems "incomplete"; Mark, Papias says, wrote down what he remembered. Clement of Alexandria adds that this material does not include the sayings of Jesus. These descriptions appear to refer to the narrative version of Q and are particularly interesting because they make no reference to the passion and death and resurrection of Jesus, nor do they refer to Mark's work as a "Gospel," a proclamation of what God had done in Jesus.

Papias also remembers that Mark "later" became Peter's "interpreter." An appropriate occasion for this would have been Peter's going to Rome (Eusebius, *Hist. eccl.* 14.6). Citing Clement, Eusebius (*Hist. eccl.* 15.1) remembers that "many" urged Mark to write down the oral teaching of Peter; I have suggested (see chap. 1) that Peter's Roman preaching was specifically focused on the passion, death, and resurrection proclamation. Jerome further remembers that this was a "short" Gospel. Since the expulsion of all Jews, including Jewish Christians, from Rome under Claudius occurred in 49 CE, the period appropriate for this period of being an "interpreter" to Peter would have been 41–49, suggesting that the QN, if earlier, could be placed in the late 30s of the first century. That many people urged Mark to write leads to two observations that support my view here. There was a need for a written account precisely in view of a sense that both Peter and Mark would soon be leaving Rome, perhaps because of the riots over "Chrestus" to which Claudius reacted in 49 with his edict of expulsion. Moreover, it seems likely that believers urged Mark in particular to write this account because they knew that he had already compiled the traditions about Jesus' ministry into the QN.

Both Jerome and Clement remember that Mark took his "completed" Gospel[1] to Egypt, specifically to Alexandria, where he formed churches (Eusebius). It seems consistent with this report to suggest the following sequence: (1) Mark had initially been from Alexandria; (2) converted to

---

1. In my view this would have been the PN in at least its basic, narrative form.

Christianity shortly after the death of Jesus; (3) learned the traditions about Jesus' teachings (the Q material) from Peter; (4) drafted them into narrative form, employing the "Son of God" category and Wisdom's presence as a Spirit in a holy person as borrowed from the Wisdom of Solomon; (5) began the PN in its basic form when in Rome with Peter; and (6) returned to his homeland after his years of being Peter's understudy, to establish the church in Alexandria. Clement of Alexandria remembers that while in Egypt Mark wrote "a more spiritual gospel." In doing so he assimilated the narrative version of Q with the passion account (QN + PN) while weaving into those texts the passages outlined in chapter 4 (above). These additions underscore Jesus' complete giving of self unto death and the necessity of disciples similarly giving of their entire lives in the face of persecution and harassment. Since the edict of Claudius is not lifted until after his death in 54, when Jews (including Jewish Christians) were allowed to return to Rome, the circumstances of 49–54 provide the appropriate context for Mark's reflection upon persecution and discipleship and his understanding of the "secret" wisdom of God revealed in Jesus' death: that discipleship means being last of all, complete selflessness in the service of others (10:45).

Hence, the author composed most of the present text of this Gospel in three separate stages during some fifteen to twenty years, as his understanding of Jesus' significance and the meaning of his death and resurrection deepened through reflection and the passing of time. If "theology" is the bringing of "faith" to the level of expression, each of the composition stages of Mark's Gospel puts the early Christian faith into narrative expression in different ways: Jesus is the eschatological prophet of the kingdom of God on whom God's Spirit rests (QN); Jesus is the Son of Man, obedient to the will of God, even unto death (PN); discipleship is the complete giving of one's self to others in obedience to the will of God — all adding up to a draft of the Gospel of Mark. "Theology" was the impulse for the Gospel of Mark; that its text matched no known "genre" should come as no surprise.

The Explanatory Glosses: Creating Our Present Text of the Gospel

A redactor naturally means explanatory phrasings to illumine a narrative that *already* exists, to make that account more accessible to an audience unfamiliar with terms or customs. The fact that a number of these in

Mark have a similarity of form suggests that an author may have made them at the same time. The list is on the facing page.[2]

Among the twenty explanatory glosses, two kinds of phrasings predominate: phrasings with γάρ (5) and phrasings with ὅ ἐστιν, sometimes followed by μεθερμηνευόμενον ... (8). The explanatory phrasings with γάρ are largely restricted to the QN material (1:16; 5:8; 9:6; 11:32), but the usage also appears in the PN account (11:13); their purpose appears to be the clarification of the narrative, making it difficult to determine when they were made. To provide a translation of customs and language, however, is clearly the intention of the ὅ ἐστιν phrasings. They appear in all three stages of the composition of Mark's Gospel. Thus, ὅ ἐστιν is in the QN at 7:11, 34, but also in the PN at 15:42 and in the modifications made when Mark joined those two accounts, at 3:17 and 12:42. Moreover, ὅ ἐστιν with μεθερμηνευόμενον ... appears both in the QN at 5:41 and in the PN at 15:22, 34. This pattern is evidence, therefore, that at least the ὅ ἐστιν phrasings were made to the text of Mark's Gospel in its third stage, when the redactor had already made modifications to assimilate the narrative version of Q with the passion account into what became, almost, our present text of Mark. These explanatory glosses bring the text of Mark to its present form.

The redactor clearly intends the ὅ ἐστιν phrasings to render intelligible the phrasings in Aramaic for a non-Jewish audience. Since Mark 7:2-4, 19 and 12:18 share that purpose, it is reasonable to attribute them to the same stage of polishing the Gospel of Mark in order to serve the needs of a now almost entirely Gentile Christian community. Although these glosses are few in number, they permit an acceptance of Mark's Gospel by the larger, universal church.[3] Consistent with this, Jerome remembers that Peter approved Mark's text, referred to as a "Gospel," for reading in the churches. The process of bringing the earliest Christian faith to the level of expression had finally given birth to a full text, the "Gospel" of Mark.

---

2. In the list QN indicates the narrative version of Q material, PN the passion account, and 3rd indicates material in third stage of assimilation of the two earlier segments of Mark's Gospel. Introductory terms are underlined.

3. The references to "the Twelve" do not appear to belong in either of the two early compositions, QN or PN. I have placed the call of the Twelve in Mark 3:16-20 at the stage of the assimilation (chap. 4, above). The basis for that would have been the consistent tradition in the passion kerygma that it was Judas, "one of the Twelve," who betrayed Jesus. It may well have been, however, that the increasing need to secure orthodoxy and authority in the early church occasioned naming the Twelve, reporting their call, and making the subsequent (few) references to them; in the Acts of the Apostles, Luke's careful narrowing of the apostleship concept witnesses to this movement to confirm authority and sound faith.

1:16	ἦσαν γὰρ ἁλεῖς	for they were fishermen	QN
2:10	λέγει τῷ παραλυτικῷ	he said to the paralytic	QN
3:17	ὅ ἐστιν...	that is, "sons of thunder"	3rd
3:30	ὅτι ἔλεγον, Πνεῦμα ἀκάθαρτον ἔχει	because they had said, "He has an unclean spirit."	QN
5:8	ἔλεγεν γὰρ αὐτῷ...	For he had been saying to him, "Unclean spirit, come out of the man"	QN
5:41	ὅ ἐστιν μεθερμηνευόμενον...	which is translated: "Little girl, I say to you, arise!"	QN
7:2–4	τοῦτ' ἔστιν...	that is, unwashed, for the Pharisees and all the Jews do not eat unless they carefully wash their hands, observing the tradition of their ancestors, nor do they eat anything from the market without sprinkling, and there are many other things that tradition has them observe, washing cups and jugs and utensils and beds.	QN
7:11	ὅ ἐστιν...	that is, "It's given"	QN
7:19	καθαρίζων πάντα τὰ βρώματα	thus making all foods "clean"	QN
7:26	ἡ δὲ γυνὴ ἦν Συροφοινίκισσα τῷ γένει	The woman was Greek, a Syrophoenician by birth.	QN
7:34	ὅ ἐστιν...	which means, "Be opened!"	QN
9:6	οὐ γὰρ ᾔδει τί ἀποκριθῇ, ἔκφοβοι γὰρ ἐγένοντο	for he did not know how to respond, for they were afraid	QN
11:13	ὁ γὰρ καιρὸς οὐκ ἦν σύκων	for it was not yet time for figs	3rd
11:32	ἅπαντες γὰρ εἶχον τὸν Ἰωάννην ὄντως προφήτης	for everyone held John to have been a prophet	QN
12:18	οἵτινες λέγουσιν ἀνάστασιν μὴ εἶναι	who say there's no resurrection	QN
12:42	ὅ ἐστιν...	which is one-fourth of a cent	3rd
13:14	ὁ ἀναγινώσκων νοείτω	Let the reader understand	3rd
15:22	ὅ ἐστιν μεθερμηνευόμενον...	which translated is "Place of a Skull"	PN
15:34	ὅ ἐστιν μεθερμηνευόμενον...	which translated is, "My God, My God! Why have you forsaken me?"	PN
15:42	ὅ ἐστιν προσάββατον	that is, the day before the Sabbath	PN

Reflection on "Mark, the Evangelist"

Perhaps it is possible to flesh out our imagining of Mark the author. We do not know where "Mark" first learned about Jesus. Negatively, we can say with some assurance that he was not native to the Judea-Galilee territory because of the improbable geographical notations in the framework material. Positively, on the other hand, we have the evidence of his familiarity with Judaism (because of the citations of the Old Testament in several places) and of his familiarity with Greek as a second language (because of the cumbersome elements of style in his text[4] and because of the strong tradition that he was the "interpreter" for Peter). We can also speak of his having a measure of affluence because writing materials were scarce and expensive,[5] and in our view, Mark continued to rework his narratives over many years. These characteristics point toward an affluent, educated Jew, in one of the major urban areas of the Roman Empire, where there would have been both a high concentration of Jews and also a Roman military garrison stationed nearby (because of the occurrence of Latinisms).

If one adds to this picture the parallels to the Wisdom of Solomon material and the wisdom background given emphasis in Mark 6:30–8:21,[6] then one might be inclined to favor Alexandria as the original home area for the author we call Mark. Tradition speaks of his going to Alexandria later in his life and of being the first bishop there, although it was likely that Christianity had already been established in Egypt by the time Claudius began as emperor in 41;[7] perhaps that was a natural choice, a return to his homeland with the endorsement of the newly emerging, hierarchical church and Peter's blessing.

Let us begin, then, with this: Mark was an educated, urban, bilingual Jew who learned the traditions about Jesus early, perhaps in the thirties, within a decade of the death of Jesus. The reasoning here is simple. Eusebius, reporting Clement of Alexandria, remembers that Mark's association with Peter was at the time of Peter's confrontation with Simon Magus, *"in the reign of Claudius"* (*Hist. eccl.* 2.14.6.). Since Claudius

---

4. Cf. Helmut Koester's description of Mark's "vulgar Koine" in his *Introduction to the New Testament* (2 vols.; Philadelphia: Fortress, 1982), 1:109.

5. Cf. J. Dewey, "From Storytelling to Written Text," *Biblical Theology Bulletin* 26 (1996): 73.

6. H. M. Humphrey, "Jesus as Wisdom in Mark," *Biblical Theology Bulletin* 19, no. 2 (1989): 48–53.

7. Cf. also Koester's comment on Acts 18:24, reporting that Apollos, the co-worker with Paul at Corinth, was an Alexandrian Jew (*Introduction*, 2:220).

became emperor in 41 and in 49, arguably, issued the edict expelling Jews from Rome, a short period of 41–49 exists for this confrontation between Peter and Simon Magus to have occurred, and we can say with confidence that Peter and Mark had to have become associates at least before 49. Clement speaks also in a way suggesting that some time elapses: Peter's preaching bests Simon; his admirers exhort Mark to put it into writing: *"nor did they cease until they had persuaded him"* (*Hist. eccl.* 2.15.1). Let us take 45, then, as an approximate and appropriate date for these events; clearly Mark would have already had to have come to Christian faith before this. And Clement reports that Mark had *already* followed Peter "for a *long* time (*Hist. eccl.* 6:14.5–6).

If one credits Papias's testimony as a witness to a time when Mark was *independent* of Peter and not yet his interpreter, but only *"later"* became his interpreter, then Mark's coming to Christianity was before 45, perhaps earlier than Claudius's accession to the throne in 41. Drawing on traditional materials, Mark writes "an account" of Jesus' words and deeds (Papias), which is not yet called a Gospel. This was arguably, a coherent narrative focused on the presence of the kingdom of God in the apocalyptic preaching of Jesus, with a striking resemblance to the interests and themes of that scholarly reconstruction of Jesus' sayings known as "Q." Indeed, it may have been precisely because of this earlier writing of Mark's that he was "later" singled out by Peter's hearers in Rome to write down the content of Peter's "gospel" preaching.

One thing is certain. What Mark "wrote down" (*Hist. eccl.* 2.14.6–7) was *not* our present canonical text. The passages in our present text exhorting disciples to "endure persecution" would have been utterly inappropriate and unintelligible to an audience for whom overt public and civil rejection had not yet been a traumatic experience. Even if the edict of 49 loomed on the horizon, that expulsion of *Jews* from Rome would not have been seen as explicitly "for my sake and the gospel's" by *all* of the early Christians there. In view of the association of Simon Magus with later gnostic views, it seems reasonable to argue that Peter's confrontation with Simon would have emphasized the human reality of Jesus — his suffering and death as well as his resurrection as the opening of the kingdom of heaven for those who would live as he had lived, a salvation promised beyond this life. In other words, what Mark wrote down in Rome was precisely the content of the "gospel" which Paul said, only a few years later, he had preached to the Corinthians: the account of the death and resurrection of the Christ. Therefore, it was Mark who, drawing upon Peter's preaching, compiled the so-called "Passion Narrative."

Certainly, both Peter and Mark would have had to leave Rome by 49 under the edict of Claudius expelling all Jews from the city. Clement's text testifies to the desire of "many" at Rome that Mark would "leave behind with them" (*Hist. eccl.* 2.15.1) a record of Peter's preaching, remembering therefore that Mark would leave Rome himself.

It is reasonable to assume that Mark and Peter separated as the regime began to enforce Claudius's edict. Peter had met his purpose: he had overcome the threat represented by Simon Magus and would move back to territories in which his lack of fluency in the Greek language would not hamper his ability to preach. This, certainly, is attested to by Paul who, in the 50s, attests to Peter's being the apostle to the "circumcised" (Gal 2:7), and by the portrayal of Peter in Acts 1–10. Mark, on the other hand, had followed Peter "for a long time," and now Peter sent Mark to his home territory of Alexandria with Peter's blessing and authority. That alone could account for the tradition that Mark became "the first bishop of the Church of Alexandria" (Jerome, *Comm. Matt.*, Prooemium, 6).

Tradition reports that Mark died in 62, several years before the death of Peter at Rome during the persecution under Nero, traditionally about 65. Several events could well have transpired in the interval between 49 and 62 and between 62 and 65. Mark, whose literary interests are well attested by his initiative in writing down, first the traditions about Jesus, and then the account of Jesus' passion, death, and resurrection, must have continued to adapt his "Gospel" to the needs of his audience (tradition remembers that he had done this in the past). He helped to develop materials on the essential meaning of Jesus' obedience to God's will for him and the implications for discipleship within the community of Christians. At some point Mark further developed and added these materials to the "Gospel" or passion account originating in Rome, leading to "a more spiritual gospel." Reflection upon the edict of expulsion in 49 might have occasioned this third stage of the textual development of Mark's Gospel; in all likelihood Mark accomplished it in the immediately following years, in the 50s of the first century. Some of the materials have a stand-alone quality as illustrations of discipleship, suggesting that the assimilation of the narrative version of Q and the passion account into something like our present text of Mark may have happened after a period of accumulating those sermon-like materials. One reason for inconsistencies in the tradition of the text[8] may well have been that it was a work in progress, as we would say; Mark could have been polishing his work even up to his death in 62.

It would have been entirely appropriate for Peter, in honoring the memory of his faithful "interpreter" and representative to Egypt, to have "ratified" Mark's Gospel to be read in all the churches (thus Jerome) sometime between 61 and 65. The explanatory glosses made to Mark's text that provide clarity to the narrative and translate Aramaic terms and Jewish customs would have an appropriate context in that event. The generally used date of 65 for the present text of Mark's Gospel is not inappropriate, therefore, but its actual composition stretches back several decades earlier.

Thus, the reconstruction of the stages of composition, based both on the characteristics of the narrative of our present text and on the patristic testimony, bring to light an individual whose role in early Christianity was significant and extensive.[9] He seems to have been an early convert, a committed Christian, the earliest historian of the tradition, the interpreter of Peter, the first bishop of one of the major early churches in Egypt, and a theologian/"mystagogue" who gave the definitive shape to the presentation of Jesus' death. That the Christian tradition has failed to remember him as such may be due in part to Rome's interest in claiming Mark for itself. I like to think, however, that this obscurity rests upon Mark's own commitment to Jesus' teaching that one must become last of all and servant of everyone (cf. Mark 9:35).

---

8. There appears to be an episode missing in 10:46 between Jesus' arriving in Jericho and his leaving the city, all in one verse. The passages Clement claims to have been in "Secret Mark" are also not in our present text.

9. Eduard Schweizer thought the fact that "Mark wrote [the Gospel] at all is the most astonishing point." See his essay "Mark's Theological Achievement," in *The Interpretation of Mark* (ed. William Telford; Philadelphia: Fortress, 1985), 42–63, esp. 43. He continues: "Mark wants to present not the words and deeds of Jesus but the gospel of Jesus Christ (the Son of God), and that in it God's history with Israel, as the prophets announced it, has come to fulfillment. Therein consists the properly theological achievement of Mark" (44).

Appendix 1

The "Mark without Q" Hypothesis

A Test Case:
Matthew's Community Discourse (Matt 18:1–35)

In the last decade Michael Goulder[1] and Mark Goodacre[2] have argued, again, that the synoptic relationships can be best resolved by recognizing that Matthew enlarged Mark's Gospel and that Luke later used both of those Gospels, a proposal that scholars have called the "Mark without Q hypothesis" (MwQH).[3] The proposal obviously seeks to discredit the long-held "Two Document Hypothesis," in which Matthew and Luke depend upon Mark and upon a collection of Jesus' sayings known cryptically as "Q." The MwQH would appear to be a consistent explanation for the parallels of sequence in Mark 8:27–9:32; Matt 16:13–17:23; and Luke 9:18–45.[4] What follows that range of material in synoptic sequence, however, constitutes a serious test of the MwQH perspective and represents a challenge to its easy dismissal of Q.

Matthew now inserts, apparently, the episode about the payment of the temple tax (Matt 17:24–27), missing in both Mark and Luke. That Luke, reading both Matthew's text and Mark's text, would not have included this is probably not an issue because the temple was long destroyed by the time he wrote, and his perspectives were of a church that had moved well beyond the Jerusalem-centered early Christian experience.

---

1. M. D. Goulder, "Is Q a Juggernaut?" *Journal of Biblical Literature* 115, no. 4 (1996): 667–81.
2. M. S. Goodacre, *The Synoptic Problem: A Way through the Maze* (Biblical Seminar; London: Sheffield Academic Press, 2001); idem, *The Case against Q: Studies in Markan Priority and the Synoptic Problem* (Harrisburg, PA: Trinity Press International, 2002).
3. Thus John S. Kloppenborg, review of M. S. Goodacre, *The Case against Q: Studies in Markan Priority and the Synoptic Problem*, *Review of Biblical Literature* 4 (October 28, 2002): 409–15. Online: http://www.bookreviews.org/pdf/1932_3151.pdf.
4. Luke does omit the Coming of Elijah material in Mark 9:9–13 and Matt 17:9–13.

Matthew returns to Mark's sequence at 18:1–5 and begins there the fourth discourse in his five-sermon complex.[5] He does so by taking advantage of a dispute among the disciples over who is the greatest, which he found at Mark 9:33–37. Matthew sharpens the focus by making it a question of who might be the greatest in "the kingdom of heaven," that broadly sketched community of those who follow Jesus' teaching (Matt 18:1–5). Luke continues to follow Mark's sequence here also and appears to prefer Mark's text over Matthew's at this point (Luke 9:46–48). Indeed, Luke continues to follow Mark in next reporting the concern of the disciples about a rival casting out demons in Jesus' name (Mark 9:38–41; Luke 9:49–50), which Matthew, on the MwQH view, must be seen as dismembering and scattering into Matt 12:30 and 10:42!

Matthew then continues with Mark's saying about temptations within the Christian community (Mark 9:42–48; Matt 18:6–9), which Luke chooses to move from this context to Luke 17:1–2; under the MwQH view it would be strange that he should do so, since both Mark and Matthew had witnessed to its present position.

At this point things become quite strange, if one adheres to the MwQH, because *both* Matthew and Luke choose to leave Mark's sequence by *omitting* Mark 9:49–50 and moving Mark's saying about salt to other contexts (Matt 5:13; Luke 14:34–35). The coincidence (!) of the common omission aside, what follows next is particularly interesting.

Matthew continues the construction of his "Community Discourse," ending characteristically with the phrasing "when Jesus had finished saying these things..." (Matt 19:1) that similarly marks the conclusion of his other discourses. Luke, on the other hand, also at this juncture composes a long section, blending materials from a variety of contexts in Matthew and Mark and including a considerable volume of materials only he reports.[6] Yet, Luke has with Matthew chosen to displace Mark's saying on salt (Mark 9:49–50) and chosen, also with Matthew, to add a

---

5. The primary focus in Goodacre's *Case against Q* is the Sermon on the Mount, Matt 5–7. He has only seven passing references to Matt 18.

6. Only Luke has the failure of Samaritan villagers to receive Jesus (9:51–56); the return of the seventy other disciples (10:17–20); the parable of the Good Samaritan (10:29–37); the welcome Mary and Martha give Jesus (10:38–42); Jesus' praise of those who hear the word of God and keep it (11:27–28); the parable of the Rich Fool (12:13–21); the lesson of the slave who didn't do what his master wanted (12:47–48); the warning about the need to have repentance in order to avoid perishing (13:1–9); Jesus' departure from Galilee (13:31–33); the parable of the Prodigal Son (15:11–32); words against hypocrisy (16:14–15); the story of Lazarus and the Rich Man (16:19–31); words about doing what one should be doing (17:7–10); the healing of ten lepers (17:11–19); and the parable of the Widow and the Judge (18:1–8).

long composition of his own at this point (Luke 9:51–18:14). Likewise, Luke agrees with Matthew to return to Mark's sequence after that, at Mark 10:1–12; Matt 19:1–12. Luke displaces the saying on divorce, but lets Mark's sequence prevail from Mark 10:13; Matt 19:13; and Luke 18:15 onward.

So, those holding to the MwQH under examination see Luke doing two things. First, he agrees with Matthew to abandon Mark's sequence in order to do something creative. Second, he chooses also to abandon Matthew's presentation, which he has in front of him. And what does he do with the materials Matthew has at this point? They are the parable of the Lost Sheep (Matt 18:10–14), On Reproving Another Believer (18:15–20), On Forgiveness (18:21–22), and the parable of the Unmerciful Servant (18:23–25). Luke reports the first item in a strikingly similar and yet different way at 15:3–7. He reduces the second to its essential and places it at 17:3. Luke again reduces the third to its essential idea and fashions it so that it balances the preceding saying and puts it at 17:4. He completely omits the parable of the Unmerciful Servant.

One must ask if all this makes sense. Under the MwQH perspective, Luke has been following Mark's sequence, as Matthew had done; he can see that Matthew has fashioned and inserted a short discourse into the Markan materials as a fuller and appropriate expansion on the problem of disunity within the Christian community. Indeed, Luke approves of three of the four items Matthew uses here. So, since he thinks those three important enough to include *elsewhere* in his Gospel, why does he *not* leave them in place here? Why does he move them into two *different* contexts when he has found them together in Matthew's Gospel? And why does he report the first in a markedly different form and the second and third in starkly abbreviated parallels?

In a small set of episodes, therefore, we can lay bare one fundamental problem of the MwQH perspective: on this basis how can one explain the manner in which Luke breaks apart the integrity of Matthew's Gospel? Whoever speaks of Luke's "literary ability"[7] as being now observable makes that "literary ability" almost unintelligible and frenetic. When Luke, comparing his text of Mark's Gospel with that of Matthew's, notices that Matthew has broken away from the Markan sequence in order to construct his Community Discourse, Luke also decides to break away at this point and construct his "Special Section" in

---

7. Thus M. Goodacre, *The Case against Q*, 189.

9:51–18:14. Of the 351 verses in that special section, 141 verses, or 40 percent of the total, have parallels in Matthew's text, and on the MwQH view Luke would have drawn them from Matthew's Gospel. What renders this incredible is that Luke would take those 141 verses from 39(!) *different* contexts in Matthew, and not one passage is in direct, continuous sequence with another. Luke makes passages widely separated in Matthew to be contiguous in his Gospel (e.g., Matt 6:25–33 and 24:43–51//Luke 12:22–34, 39–46); he separates passages found close together in Matthew (e.g., materials of Matt 23 appear in Luke 11:37–52 and 13:34–35). Such a manner of composing can hardly be imagined as placing a pencil in one scroll (Mark's) to hold one's place while unrolling the other (Matthew's) in order to scan for the places he had left uncopied, some twenty-five different contexts to that point. Hence, the cut-and-paste method of composition is difficult for us to imagine here.

The materials in Matthew's Community Discourse and what Luke allegedly has done with the materials of Matthew's Gospel at this point just do not support the suggestion that the MwQH simplifies our understanding of synoptic relationships. Rather than leading to a simple explanation for the parallels between Matthew and Luke, this hypothesis forces one to imagine a most contrived and difficult process of editing of Matthew's text in order to explain what Luke has constructed in 9:51–18:14 in lieu of Matthew's Community Discourse.[8] It seems a bit early, accordingly, to proclaim the MwQH as sounding the "death knell" of Q.

Other Considerations

Rather than simplifying synoptic relationships, the Mark without Q Hypothesis (that Matthew expanded Mark and that Luke uses both Mark and Matthew as sources for his Gospel) seems to leave many questions.

There are materials in Mark which are not in Matthew (Mark 1:35–38; 4:26–29; 8:22–26; 12:41–44). Luke 3:42–43 follows the first

---

8. In fact, the classic Two Document Hypothesis seems preferable here. On that hypothesis, Q would have made available to Matthew something like the block of short, pointed sayings that appears in Luke 17:1–2, 3–4. Matthew's desire to expand Mark into a sermon would explain both his using those sayings in Matt 18 and his substituting them for Mark's words on salt (9:49–50). It seems far more comprehensible that Matthew would have expanded the succinctness of the sayings in Q 17:1–2, 3–4 to develop his interests in "church" than that Luke, with his apparent churchly interest as manifest in the Acts of the Apostles, would have abbreviated those sayings from Matt 18:6–9, 15–20, 21–22. Expansion in order to articulate a theme is far more understandable than compression for brevity when such a compression at that location eliminates the theme in which one otherwise is obviously interested.

(Mark 1:35–38), and Luke 21:1–4 parallels the last (Mark 12:41–44). So on the MwQH *both* Matthew and Luke have *chosen* to omit Mark 4:26–29 and 8:22–26. Are these just strange coincidences?

Again, on the same basis Luke must have chosen quite deliberately not to include a number of texts that he found in Matthew, although they have no parallels in Mark's Gospel: Matt 6:1–4, 5–8, 16–18; 7:6; 13:24–30, 33, 36–43, 44–46, 47–50, 51–52; 17:24–27; 18:23–35; 20:1–16; 25:31–46; 27:3–10, 62–66. For each of these the supporters of MwQH must find an explanation for Luke's decision to omit what he had in front of him in Matthew's text.

The problem of Luke's presenting an entirely different Infancy Narrative from the one put forward by Matthew needs explanation as well. So, too, does Luke's omission of Jesus' words about the nearness of the kingdom of God, which open Jesus' ministry in both Mark 1:15 and Matt 4:17.

There are other omissions that also cry out for explanations. Why the omission of Thaddeus in the list of the Twelve (cf. Luke 6:14–15, with parallels in Mark 3:16–18 and Matt 10:2–4)? Why the omission of Matt 6:1–4, On Almsgiving, toward which Luke would have been supportive given his advocacy of the poor in Luke 6:20, 24 and elsewhere? We could ask similar questions for all the texts in Matthew's Gospel that speak to themes in which Luke has an apparent interest, as we can judge that interest from the materials he has included in his Gospel and in the Acts of the Apostles.

The traditional Two Document Hypothesis does seem to handle one text better than any other solution to the Synoptic Problem; that is Matt 16:17–19, where Jesus promises to Peter the keys of the kingdom and gives him the power of binding and loosing within the church. That text and the repeated reference to "church" in Matt 18:15–20 do not occur in Luke's Gospel. Nevertheless, Luke is noticeably interested in the church; the word "church" (ἐκκλησία) occurs twenty-three times in the Acts of the Apostles, and Peter's role in that church is prominent in its opening chapters. Why the omission? For this author, those twin omissions by Luke can find no plausible explanation and are a major weakness of the MwQH.

In summary, therefore, the consequences of the MwQH in the Gospel texts themselves do not support the premise. The MwQH requires that we admire Luke's literary creativity in composing his Gospel by breaking apart the five-sermon complex he found in Matthew. Yet we have difficulty in imagining exactly how in the world he would be able to do that, given just the example of Matthew's Community Discourse and the similarly placed Lukan Special Section.

Furthermore, if one turns from what we see that Luke *includes* of Matthew's and Mark's Gospels to what he, presumably, chooses to *omit* from them, we must seek an explanation for every instance of conscious omission. Is a consistent set of explanations possible? The benchmark would appear to be the characteristic interests of Luke as they appear in his Gospel and the Acts of the Apostles, and yet a number of omissions do not seem explainable in that way.

And so, a certain few scholars will not be able easily to overturn the Two Source Hypothesis that has served biblical studies well for over three-quarters of a century. For this author the sayings material known as Q remains a stable tradition in early Christianity, which Matthew and Luke independently appropriated for their Gospels. There are, moreover, two aspects to the traditional Q hypothesis that make it preferable: the extent to which blocks of materials alleged to be "Q" stay together in *Luke's* sequence, and that an overall coherence results for Q from that arrangement.

At this point the "Q" hypothesis appears simpler and therefore stronger than the MwQH offered in its place.

Appendix 2

Assessing the Quest for a Proto-Mark

For over three-quarters of a century biblical scholarship has generally embraced the so-called Two Source, or Two Document, Hypothesis according to which the Gospels of Matthew and Luke derived their materials from the Gospel of Mark and that collection of Jesus' sayings that came to be named Q. The affirmation of Matthew and Luke depending upon the text of the Gospel of Mark, however, has always had a nagging problem, a thorn in its side, as Marie-Émile Boismard observed:[1] those places where the text of Matthew and the text of Luke do not follow Mark's text, but amazingly differ from it in the same way. Delbert Burkett puts it well:

> Critics of the two-document hypothesis find its Achilles' heel in the minor agreements of Matthew and Luke against Mark in the triple tradition. In this theory Matthew and Luke supposedly copied Mark independently, yet in numerous places they agree with each other against Mark. It is customary to categorize such agreements as "major" or "minor." The two-document hypothesis explains the major agreements by noting that Mark and Q sometimes preserved the same story or saying. The major agreements then would be places where Matthew and Luke abandoned Mark to follow a parallel tradition in Q. The minor agreements, where no parallel tradition from Q is in evidence, have been more problematic for the theory.[2]

---

1. M.-É. Boismard, *L'Évangile de Marc: Sa préhistoire* (ÉBib, n.s., 26; Paris: Gabalda, 1994), 9.
2. D. Burkett, *Rethinking the Gospel Sources: From Proto-Mark to Mark* (New York: T & T Clark, 2004), 1.

One approach taken to explain these agreements against Mark's text has been to posit an earlier version of Mark, employed by Matthew and Luke and different from the present and actual canonical text of Mark's Gospel. And so the quest began for an earlier version of Mark's Gospel, perhaps a less complete and subsequently redacted version of Mark: a "Proto-Mark."

The most recent effort in this direction is that of Burkett, and so we start there. His conclusions are simply stated:

> No one Synoptic served as a source for either of the other two. All theories of Markan priority, Matthean priority, and Lukan priority thus start from a wrong premise.... Instead,... all three Synoptics drew on a set of earlier written sources that have been lost.[3]

His approach is a comparative analysis of the Synoptic Gospels. Thus, for example, he studies the "Markan Redaction" absent from Matthew and Luke and in a series of tables shows that Markan materials with distinctive vocabulary and themes are missing in the Gospels of Matthew and Luke; consequently "The gospel of Mark did not serve as a source for either Matthew or Luke."[4] A comparison of the sources common to Mark and Matthew yields, Burkett believes, a large common sequence of material that "as it includes that greater part of Mark — and no material from Q, M, or L — it could be considered an earlier version of Mark, a Proto-Mark"[5] that he calls Proto-Mark A to distinguish it from other sequences that he will designate with the letters "Proto-Mark B" (materials shared with Luke) and "C" (materials shared with Matthew and Luke). Additionally, he identifies a miracle/mission source shared with Matthew and Luke, and a parable discourse shared with Luke.[6]

But the picture of the sources Mark employs is "complicated by the fact that several of these sources overlapped."[7] He acknowledges that "this study postulates the existence of several lost documents from which the extant gospels drew their material, just as the two-document hypothesis postulates the existence of a lost document."[8] There is no embarrassment in that multiplicity of lost documents because "the simpler

---

3. Ibid., 5.
4. Ibid., 42.
5. Ibid., 77.
6. For this summary, cf. ibid., 224.
7. Ibid., 224.
8. Ibid., 263.

theories have been found wanting, and it is time to move on to the more complex."⁹

This summary of Burkett's thesis is much too short to give full appreciation to the abundance of analytical detail presented, yet it suffices to indicate that here the "quest" for the Proto-Mark behind the Gospel of Mark has generated at least two Proto-Marks and several other sources. The nagging problem of the agreements of Matthew and Luke against Mark (in our view perhaps best explained by those evangelists knowing earlier editions of the materials Mark will ultimately produce as his "Gospel"!) has led to a hypothesis far more complex than the challenged Two Source Hypothesis. What this summary of Burkett's work also indicates is the absence of concern for the narrative integrity of these materials and for Mark's purpose in conflating them into the present text of the Gospel of Mark. It is an intriguing analysis, but it leaves one with no sense of the soul and convictions of the persons behind these sources, nor of the evangelist Mark himself.

The reconstruction of a Proto-Mark by M.-É. Boismard a decade earlier (1994) begins with quite different assumptions and yields a single Proto-Mark behind the present text of the canonical Gospel of Mark. The picture Boismard sketches of the traditions about Jesus in early Christianity derives from his analysis of the Synoptic Gospels.[10]

> The aim was to distinguish several levels of redaction in each of the fundamental traditions. Thus, in the Matthean tradition, the oldest was that which we have called Document A, probably translated from Aramaic (Aramaic Matthew). From this Document A developed a more complex gospel, intermediate Matthew, which had incorporated a certain number of materials taken especially from what the Two Source theory calls the Q source. Then this intermediate Matthew was taken over and completed by an ultimate Redactor in order to give birth to the gospel of Matthew in its present form. The Markan tradition looks back to a certain Document B, itself dependent upon Document A (or perhaps the Aramaic Matthew). From this Document B developed a more complete gospel, intermediate Mark, which would have in many respects fused

---

9. Ibid., 263.
10. M.-É. Boismard, A. Lamouille, and P. Sandevoir, *Synopse des quatre Évangiles en français*, vol. 2, *Commentaire* (2nd ed.; Paris: Éditions du Cerf, 1972).

materials coming from Documents A and B. Finally this intermediate Mark would have been taken over and completed a little to form the gospel of Mark in its present form. This ultimate Redactor of the gospel of Mark had a style similar to Luke's, hence we have given the name "Marco-Lukan" to that Redactor.[11]

But Boismard's analysis of a Proto-Mark really depends upon his later study of the Acts of the Apostles and his sense that elements of Lukan style are conspicuously evident in the text of the Gospel of Mark. "As a consequence, the difference between intermediate Mark and the present text of Mark is very much more marked; on the other hand, the difference between intermediate Mark and Document B tends to be diminished to the point where one could ask if it is any more necessary to distinguish the two."[12] Now Boismard sees the influence of Matthean and Lukan traditions on the final Markan redaction.

Thus, working with the *present texts* of the Gospels of Matthew, Mark, and Luke, Boismard argues that our canonical Gospel of Mark acquired its form when an earlier Proto-Mark, missing a passion narrative, was redacted by an editor employing elements of Lukan style. Many passages in the present text of Mark betray those Lukan characteristics and hence are redactional, not part of that earlier Proto-Mark, which in its turn was dependent upon an "intermediate" form of the Gospel of Matthew and earlier Markan materials.

As an example of Boismard's reasoning, let us take the Cleansing of the Leper account (Mark 1:40–45; Matt 8:1–4; Luke 5:12–16).[13] A Matthean account underlies this Markan story because the expression "stretching out his hand" is found nowhere else in Mark but is found in Matt 12:49; 14:31; and 26:51. It has been added by Matthew to the parallels with Mark and Luke in the first and last of those passages and is unique to Matthew in 14:31. Moreover, it is possible to recover from Mark's text elements of an earlier account unknown by Matthew and Luke; these are found in the passage's introduction (Mark 1:40a), which differs markedly from those of Matthew and Luke; in the reaction of Jesus, for which Boismard chooses to use the variant "angered" (1:41a); and in how Jesus sends the leper away (1:43). Boismard believes that the Marco-Lukan redactor fused the two accounts into the present text.

---

11. My translation of Boismard, *L'Évangile de Marc*, 1.
12. Again, my translation of ibid., 2.
13. Ibid., 68–72.

We should, however, recognize how Boismard makes several assumptions here. The first is that one can use the *present text* of the Gospel of Matthew, which in Boismard's view is the work of a final redactor of intermediate Matthew, as evidence for an earlier Matthean account the Marco-Lukan redactor would have used. The second is that we can see Proto-Mark in the phrasings of Mark's present text that are without parallels in Matthew's and Luke's present texts. And yet another assumption is that these earlier materials, the Matthean account and the Proto-Mark account, were static *documents,* subject to editing, and not materials in a fluid tradition.

These assumptions and arguments have led Boismard to a quite strange reconstruction of this account in Proto-Mark: A leper comes to Jesus, calling out to him and falling to his knees (Mark 1:40a); Jesus' reaction is anger (Boismard chooses the variant ὀργισθείς instead of the usual expression of compassion, σπλαγχνισθείς, v. 41a); and Jesus sternly admonishes the man and sends him away at once (v. 43). This reconstruction, despite Boismard's arguments, appears quite arbitrary in that he lets Proto-Mark omit the balance of v. 40, most of verses 41 and 42, and verse 44 — even though all three Synoptic Gospels witness to them.

Perhaps Boismard has too quickly applied his thesis of a Marco-Lukan redactor's editing of a Proto-Mark as an explanation for the differences between the Matthean and Markan texts of the Cleansing of the Leper, without sufficiently weighing the parallels in Luke's account. Here in a number of ways Luke agrees with Matthew against Mark: (1) neither Gospel reports Jesus giving a reaction to the leper's petition (Matt 8:3; Luke 5:13); (2) both choose the participle form of the verb ("saying," λέγων) over the indicative before Jesus' verbal response (Matt 8:3; Luke 5:13); (3) both prefer εὐθέως instead of the adverb found in Mark (Matt 8:3; Luke 5:13); (4) both have no mention of the narrative comment that the healed leper is "sent away" (cf. Matt 8:3–4 and Luke 5:13–14 with Mark 1:43). Could we here have Matthew and Luke witnessing to a different version of the Cleansing of the Leper tradition, one for which the present text of Mark is *either* the source *or* a redacted version? It therefore appears that Boismard has moved too quickly to identify the content of Proto-Mark at this point.

Boismard's Proto-Mark is a reconstruction dependent upon his theory of sources behind the Synoptic Gospels, a reconstruction admirably based upon very careful and detailed analyses of the present texts of those

Gospels. Yet the Proto-Mark that analysis discloses is an odd entity. It has no passion narrative, as Boismard sees it, ending at 14:25; and yet with the passion predictions of Mark 8:31 and 9:31, his Proto-Mark does anticipate an account of the passion (10:33–34 is missing). Boismard's explanation for the absence of a passion narrative seems strained:

> It seems certain to us that Proto-Mark did not contain the narratives of the passion and of the resurrection. But is that conceivable? Don't these narratives express the essential element of the Christian faith?... Here is the hypothesis which we propose to justify this anomaly. Proto-Mark ended with the account of the institution of the eucharist (Mark 14:22–25) which the early Christian communities renewed each week, on the "Day of the Lord" (cf. Luke 22:19). This eucharist was a memorial of the passion of Christ and the "Day of the Lord" commemorated his resurrection. During the liturgical practice, one had accordingly to read the texts recounting the passion and the resurrection of the Christ.... In ending his gospel with the narrative of the institution of the eucharist, didn't Proto-Mark want to say to his readers: it is not useful to tell you how the Christ died and was raised since you read the account of it each Sunday, within the liturgy?[14]

From a narrative point of view, to anticipate an account of the death and resurrection with the predictions of Jesus in 8:31 and 9:31, without actually providing that account, would lead the reader to a sense of incompleteness; is that not why Boismard felt the need to explain its absence? Indeed, using Boismard's hypothesis that the readers of Mark did not need the passion narrative because of their weekly liturgical commemoration of the death and resurrection of Jesus, why was the passion narrative composed at all? This reconstruction of Proto-Mark is certainly an odd entity.

Moreover, in just the first six chapters of Mark, 141 verses or parts of verses of the present text of Mark are not to be found in Proto-Mark. That constitutes 57 percent of the total 248 verses in those six chapters. By Boismard's own admission, Proto-Mark was substantially different from our present text of the Gospel of Mark,[15] and the enigmatic, and

---

14. Again, my translation of ibid., 242–43.
15. Ibid., 2: "La différence entre le Marc-intermédiaire et le Marc actuel est beaucoup plus marquée."

otherwise unknown, "Marco-Lukan" redactor has had much responsibility for our present text of the Gospel of Mark, creatively reshaping Proto-Mark into something quite different, as Boismard's presentation of the Cleansing of the Leper account shows.

In my study of the composition history of the Gospel of Mark, I do not have in mind a dialogue with the "thorn in the side" (see above) of the Two Source Theory. That hypothesis has "worked," as Norman Perrin said in a private conversation over three decades ago; he observed that the fruitful results from a redaction-critical approach to the Gospels strengthen the hypothesis. Still, what I propose in this study might lead us to reexamine the problem of Matthew's and Luke's agreements against Mark's present text. In my view, Mark composed the parts of his text we have identified as a narrative version of Q (QN) and a passion narrative (PN), yet at different times and originally independent of each other. Tentatively, I suggest that the QN, to which Papias seems to allude, was earlier than the PN, to which Clement alludes. Indeed, it might well have been that, since believers knew Mark had already composed a narrative of things Jesus said and did in his ministry, they later urged him also to provide for the Roman community an account of Peter's witness and preaching about the death and resurrection of Jesus, as Clement says.

In any event, in my view it would have been entirely likely that these two narratives won a measure of independent circulation among the early Christian communities, and that Mark continued to refine his own texts of those narratives as he kept using them personally. Certainly Mark chose to edit those texts in a significant way in order to integrate the QN and the PN and produce a narrative of the "good news" (Mark 1:1), which disclosed the secret of the kingdom of God (8:27–10:45). Subsequently he would have expanded that material to provide illustrations of the discipleship necessary to live according to that secret wisdom. In my view, during the composition history of the Gospel of Mark, the author developed elements of our present text of Mark over time; until the last editorial additions of the explanatory glosses, it was the work of the single person we call Mark. That Matthew and Luke can agree together against Mark might have happened because they knew of, or remembered, those publicly circulated narratives that Mark had not yet combined into the present text of his Gospel. For example, the elements of Jesus' compassion (σπλαγχνισθείς, Mark 1:41a) and the sending away of the healed leper in order to preserve the effort at secrecy (1:43) might arguably be redactions by Mark to his own, earlier, and simpler account as now reflected in Matthew and Luke.

In short, here lies the difference between my view and the critiqued reconstructions: Burkett and Boismard propose that an unknown redactor edits unattested documents and produces Proto-Mark(s) for unspecified purposes. I, on the other hand, urge that the present text of Mark results from the ever-maturing theological reflection of the Christian tradition's first evangelist, Mark.

Index

Acts
  2   16
  3   16
  18:24   24n31
  Peter portrayed in, 1–10   146
Acts of the Apostles, 17, 142n3, 152n8, 153, 154, 158
Adam
  disobedience of, 113, 114n29
  Jesus contrasted with, 91, 92, 93
  second, Christology, 96
Alexandria. *See also* Egypt
  association of Wisdom of Solomon with, 50
  Christianity in, 24n31
  death and burial of Mark at, 30, 31, 35, 36, 37
  Jerome in, 28
  Mark in, 28, 33, 88, 144, 146, 147
  spiritual Gospel from, 38
Alexandrian churches, 28, 31, 32, 36, 140
"Amazing Grace," 41n11
Anderson, Hugh, 14
Annianus, as successor of Mark, 27, 30
Anti-Marcionite Prologue, 21, 24
Aramaic phrasings, 5, 9, 38, 50n26, 142, 147

baptism, 14, 44n21, 45, 85n37, 118, 125, 135
Barabbas, 100, 108, 109, 113
Bethany
  anointing in, 102
  Jesus retreats to, 130
  motif of residence in, 132
biblical scholarship
  contemporary, 94
  focus on Mark by, 1
  redaction criticism among, 3
  on relationship between Mark and Q, 41

biblical scholarship (*continued*)
  Second Gospel according to, 2
  Two-Document Hypothesis embraced by, 39, 149, 155, 156
Black, C. Clifton, 13n16
Boismard, Marie-Émile, 6, 7, 155, 157–62
Brown, Raymond, 94, 95n11
Burkett, Delbert, 6, 155, 156, 157, 162

Caesar, knights of, 20, 21
Carpocratians, teachings of, 33
centurion, 103, 135, 136
chreia (useful anecdotes), 4, 84, 87
Christ. *See also* Jesus
  at Alexandria, 30
  Jesus as, 13, 34, 96, 100, 101, 122
  obedient, 93, 94
  recordings of, 11
  references to, 49
  suffering of, 7
  testimonies concerning, 20, 21
  title of, 118
Christian church, 2, 40
Christian community, 40, 127, 137, 138, 142, 150. *See also* Jewish-Christian community
Christian faith, 7, 24n31, 141, 142, 145, 160
Christianity
  in Alexandria, 24n31
  converts introduction to, 124
  early, 26, 89, 90, 96, 114, 118, 139, 147, 154, 157
  Egyptian, 24n31, 50, 144
  history of, 41
  Mark's conversion to, 141–42, 145
  Paul's theology of, 90–91, 93, 137
Christology
  low, 49, 50
  messianic, 14, 49, 50
  reflected in Mark, 89–93
  reflected in Phil and Paul, 102
  second Adam, 96

church(es). *See also* Alexandrian churches; Christian church; Coptic Church
  contemporary, 7
  dependence on second-generation Gospels, 24
  Gospel authorized to read in, 37
  role of Peter, 153
  Roman and Alexandrian, 28
  scriptures for, reading, 19
  teachings of, 22
  testimonies of, fathers, 9, 140
  testimonies of, writers, 36
  witness of, fathers, 10–36
Claudius, 16, 19, 25, 37, 138, 140, 141, 144, 146
Cleansing of the Leper account, 158–59, 162
Clement of Alexandria
  conflicting testimony of, 21–24
  Eusebius on, 15, 17, 32
  letter to Theodore, 20, 32, 33, 35n47, 36
  on Magus, 18
  on Mark and Peter, 30
  Papias in agreement with, 18
  recap of, 20–21
  secret Gospel and, 32–35, 124, 147n8
  testimony of, 6, 15–20, 26, 32, 37, 138, 140, 141, 144, 145, 161
  tradition not mentioned by, 28
Commentary on Matthew (Jerome), 27, 28
Community Discourse, of Matthew, 149–54
composition. *See also* Gospel of Mark; Mark
  history of, 5–7, 9, 33–38, 117n1, 123–24, 161
  narrative characteristics of, 25, 32
  Papias on, 13n16
  process, 139–41
  revisions of, 38, 93
  stages of, 117, 141, 142, 147
  time frame for, 18–19, 31
Coptic Church, 36
1 Corinthians (1 Cor)
  1   26
  1:30   90n1
  15   93
  15:21–23   91
  15:45–49   91
  Romans aligned with, 92
  theology of Paul in, 137
Crossan, John Dominic, 35n48

Damasus, Pope, 28
Daniel (Dan), 7   115

data, accuracy of, 3
De viris illustribus (Jerome), 29
Diaspora, 50, 114
discipleship
  commentary of, 122
  core essence of, 127
  emphasis on, within text, 6, 118
  focus of, 102n26, 120, 138
  in Galilee, 101–2
  illustrations of, 161
  implications for, 136, 146
  to Jesus, 124
  lessons for, 7, 132
  model for, 135
  narratives exemplifying, 37
  nature of, 5
  negative portrayals of, 34, 133, 134
  paradigms of, 117
  persecution and, 141
  Peter's failed, 103, 123, 134
  in QN, 49
Doge Giustiniano Participazio, 35
Donahue, John, 37, 137, 138

Ecclesiastical History (Eusebius), 10, 26, 30
Egypt. *See also* Alexandria
  Christianity taken to, 24n31, 50, 144
  completed Gospel taken to, 138, 140
  Gospel written in Rome and, 36
  Mark in, 9, 19, 24–27, 32, 33, 35
Egyptian connection, 24–25
the Elder, 10, 11, 14, 15
the elect, 83, 84, 87, 90, 92, 93, 116, 132
Ellis, E. Earle, 9n3, 12
eschatological discourse, 37, 45, 129, 132
Eusebius
  on Clement, 15, 17, 32
  history of Magus recounted by, 18
  Jerome's reference to, 30
  preface addressed to, 28
  testimony of, 25–27, 144
  testimony of Papias cited by, 10
  tradition in, 19
Exegesis of the Lord's Oracles (Papias), 10
explanatory glosses, 141–43

Feast of Unleavened Bread, 97, 98, 103, 104, 112
Fleddermann, Harry, 41, 43n19
form criticism, 2, 5
fragmentation, 2, 4

Galilee
  discipleship in, 101–2
  Jesus followed by women from, 116
  prediction of presence in, 102–3
  return to, 103
Garden of Eden, 86, 91, 92
Garden of Gethsemane, 96, 98, 99, 105, 113, 114
Genesis (Gen)
  1:27 114n29
  5:1 91
Gentiles, 95, 99, 102, 116, 136, 142
Georgi, Dieter, 112
God
  kingdom of, 26, 42, 44, 45, 47–49, 84–87, 90, 94, 117, 119, 120, 121, 127, 132, 136, 138, 141, 145, 153, 161
  will of, 42, 56, 84–87, 90, 92, 93, 98, 99, 113–16, 122–24, 126, 128, 130, 136, 137, 141, 146
Goodacre, Mark, 6n15, 149
Gospel of John. *See* John
Gospel of Luke, 1, 3, 39, 112. *See also* Luke
Gospel of Mark. *See also* composition; Mark
  assembling, 117–35
  clarification from, 9
  evidence written in Rome, 24–25, 36, 137
  foreshadowing events as element of, 121
  literary complexity of, 5
  Matthew's copy of, 2n6
  origination of, 5
  Peter authorizes, 37
  recurring motifs in, 2
  short, 31
  theological nuances of, 5
  time frame for composition of, 18–19, 31
  writing of, 11–15
Gospel of Matthew, 1, 3, 39, 44n21. *See also* Matthew
Gospel of Thomas, 35n48
Gospel, secret, 32–35, 37, 123, 124, 126
Goulder, Michael, 149

Hellenistic rhetoric, 84n30
Hellenistic world, 87–88
Hellenistic youth, 4
Holy Spirit, 23, 44, 51, 56
Hypotyposes (Clement), 15, 17, 18

Irenaeus, 22, 23, 24

James, 25–26, 29, 84, 85n37, 125, 127, 132
Jerome, 27–32, 37, 138, 142

Jesus, 6. *See also* Christ; Passion Narrative (PN); Q; Son of Man; teacher
  Adam contrasted with, 91, 92, 93
  as agent of Wisdom, 90
  baptism of, 14, 45, 85n37, 135
  burial of, in Mark 15:42–46 101
  chreia attributed to, 84
  death and resurrection of, 13, 16, 17, 26, 27, 34, 89–103, 121, 124, 127, 132, 135–37, 139, 140, 145, 160, 161
  in Decapolis, 88
  discipleship to, 124
  dramatization of rejection of, 99–101
  eternal life teachings of, 49
  ethic taught by, 87
  history of, 1, 2
  as Holy Son of God, 46–47
  interpretation of, 41
  in Jerusalem, 85
  John the Baptist career followed by, 90
  John's motif of, 112
  knowledge of scriptures, 130
  life of, 39
  Mark's knowledge of, 144
  parables spoken by, 44, 56, 58, 67
  Peter's acclamation of, 122
  petition for body of, 111
  Pharisees as opponents to, 118
  before Pilate, 100, 108–9, 134
  portrayals of, 45, 136
  protest of, in Mark 10:18 26
  reference to, as Lord, 13, 14
  retreats to Bethany, 130
  secret of God's plan for, 35
  secret sayings from, 35n48
  story line focused on, 42
  as teacher, 40, 85n40, 90, 128
  women as followers of, 116
Jewish community, 85, 138
Jewish customs, 9, 30, 38, 102, 117n1, 147
Jewish Scriptures, 84, 87, 130
Jewish wisdom, 40, 114
Jewish-Christian community, 87, 112, 113, 114, 116
John
  as disciple of Lord, 23
  Mark 14:1–30 paralleled by,
    13:1–38 97n15
  motif of Jesus in, 112
John the Baptist
  death of, 121, 122, 132
  illustration of, 136
  Jesus follows career of, 90

Joseph of Arimathea, 116
Josephus, 25, 26
Judaeus, Philo. *See* Philo the Jew
Judaism, 50, 112, 136–37, 144
Judas
  betrayal of, 34, 94, 97–99
  as one of Twelve, 103, 106, 120, 142n3

kerygmatic proclamation, 95, 96, 139
Kloppenborg, John, 40, 43n19

Lake, Kirsopp, 11
Lane, William, 24n32
Latinisms, 5, 24
literary criticism, contemporary, 3
"Lord's Prayer," 86
love, principles centered on, 81, 84–87, 91, 129
Lukan Special Section, 154
Luke. *See also* Gospel of Luke
9: 31	22
9:18–45	43, 149
9:51–18:14	43, 152
17:1–2	150
18:15	151

  dependence upon Mark and Q by, 149
  Jerome's reference to, 30
  Markan materials referenced by, 151, 156, 158
  Matthew and, 40, 155, 161
  Q sayings sequence by, 40
  sources used by, 6n15
  temple text missing in, 149
  text in Matthew omitted by, 153
  text of Mark parallels in, 7

Magus, Simon
  Clement on, 18
  Peter's confrontation with, 19, 144, 145, 146
Manson, T. W., 21
Marco-Lukan redactor, 161
Mark. *See also* composition; Gospel of Mark; Gospel, secret; narrative version of Q (QN); Passion Narrative (PN); Proto-Mark Hypothesis; Q
1:1	26, 118
1:2–13:32	42, 43, 44–48
1:15	84n32
1:21	43n19
1:24	85n38
2:10	48n24
2:13–3:6	48n24, 118–19, 136

Mark (*continued*)
3:7	143
3:11	85n39
3:14a	119–20
3:16–20	119–20
3:17	9n1
3:35	84n36
4:10–20	120–21, 136, 137
4:21	43n19
4:26–29	153
5:41	9n1
6:14–29	9n2, 121–22
6:30–8:21	144
7:2–4	9n1, 142
7:11	9n1
7:19	142
7:34	9n1
8:22–26	117, 153
8:27–9:32	149
8:27–33	101, 122–25, 160
8:38	40
9:9–13	125
9:30–32	101, 125–26, 160
9:33–37	150
10:1–12	151
10:32–34	35n47, 101, 126–28
10:35–45	35n47, 126–28
10:46–52	117, 128–29
11:1–10	44n20, 129–30
11:11b–15a	129–30, 143
11:18–27	44n20, 129–30
12:1–12	130–31
12:18	142
12:29–31	84n34
12:34	84n35
12:41–44	9n2, 131–32, 143
13	44n20, 90, 93, 115, 129
13:14	143
13:20	84n31
13:22	84n31
13:26–27	84n31, 84n33
14:1	97–99, 112, 113
14:1–30 paralleled by John 13:1–38	97n15
14:3–9	9n2, 97n15, 132–33
14:10	97–99
14:12–42	48n23, 48n25, 96, 97–99, 103, 112, 114, 120–21, 133–34
14:43	113
14:50	103
14:53–15:32	100, 113
14:54	134
14:55	113

Mark (*continued*)
14:60-61   113, 114
14:62   48n24, 96, 115
14:63   113
14:66-72   134
15:1   113
15:3   113
15:10   102
15:11   113
15:16   112
15:22   9n1, 102, 112
15:31   113
15:34   9n1, 102, 112, 113
15:38-39   116, 134-35, 136
15:42   9n1, 102
15:43   48n23
16:7   103
18:1-5   150
 in Alexandria, 28, 33, 88, 144, 146, 147
 burial of Jesus in, 15:42-46   101
 change in ministry of, 27
 characteristic features of, 14:1-16:8 93-94
 Christology reflected in, 89-93
 community reflected by, 112-16, 135-38
 conversion to Christianity by, 141-42, 145
 death and burial of, 30, 31, 35, 36, 37
 dramatization of betrayal in, 97-99
 in Egypt, 9, 19, 24-27, 32, 33, 35
 with Egyptian Christianity, 50
 focus on, 1
 healing of blind man in 8:22-26   26
 high priests referenced in, 11:27 97n14
 history of interest in, 1-5
 Irenaeus on, 22, 23, 24
 Luke and Matthew's dependence on Q
   and, 149
 Matthew and Luke against, 155, 161
 modern day interest in, 5-7
 outline for materials in, 15:1-32   99
 parallels in Luke and Matthew, 7
 passion prediction within, 94, 95, 126-28,
   160
 persecution in 13   5
 Peter and, 11-21, 29-30, 36, 145, 146
 present text of, 5-7, 9, 13, 14, 18, 24-26,
   34, 36, 37, 46, 87n41, 89, 93, 96, 101,
   102, 117, 118, 122, 125, 126, 129,
   139-42, 141-43, 145-47, 157-62
 protest of Jesus in 10:18   26
 Psalm 22:1 in, 15:34   113
 purpose of, 14:32-42   113
 quadrans of 12:42   5
 reflection on, as evangelist, 144-47

Mark (*continued*)
 relationship between Q and, 41
 in Rome, 9, 14, 19, 22, 37
 second person elements in, 13   132, 136
 secondary material in, 14:1-16:8   102
 Son of Man in, 48n24
 temple text missing in, 149
 traditional material compiled by, 1-2
 verb-less phrasing in, 1:1   42
Mark without Q hypothesis (MwQH),
   149-54
Markan materials, 44, 48, 151, 156, 158
Markan tradition, 43, 157
Martin, Ralph, 11, 12n12
Matthew (Matt). *See also* Gospel of Matthew
 12:49   158
 14:31   158
 16:13-17:23   149
 16:17-19   153
 18:15-20   153
 19:1-12   151
 26:51   158
 Community Discourse of, 149-54
 dependence upon Mark and Q by, 149
 distribution of Gospel among Hebrews, 23
 Gospel of Mark copy of, 2n6
 Luke and, 40, 155, 161
 Markan materials referenced by, 151, 156,
   158
 as Papias' standard, 14
 sources used by, 6n15
 text of Mark parallels in, 7
monastic community, 32
MwQH. *See* Mark without Q hypothesis
mystagogue, 33, 34

narrative criticism, 4, 5
narrative version of Q (QN). *See also* Q
 1:1   117
 1:2-45   50-54
 1:16-20   119, 143
 2:1-12   54-55, 118, 122, 143
 2:13-3:6   122
 3:6   121
 3:7-12   55, 119
 3:10-15   55, 119
 3:21-34   55-56, 86, 119, 143
 4:1-9   56-57, 120
 4:21-33   57-58, 120
 4:35-41   58-59
 5:1-43   59-62, 142, 143
 6:1-13   62-63, 121
 6:30-8:21   63-65, 119, 121

narrative version of Q (QN). *(continued)*

7:1-15	65-67, 142, 143
7:17-37	67-69, 142, 143
8:1-26	69-71, 123, 128, 132
8:27-10:45	123, 124, 126, 129
8:27-33	122, 127, 128
8:34-9:1	71, 122, 124, 125, 127
9:1-5	71-72
9:6	143
9:7	72
9:8	72
9:14-29	72-73, 125, 126
9:31	127
9:33-43	73-74, 125, 129
9:45	74
9:47-50	74-75
10:1-31	75-78, 127, 129
10:32	129
10:46-52	123, 129
11:11	78
11:15-17	78
11:27-34	78-79, 134, 143
12:13-34	79-81, 85, 143
12:34	130, 131
12:37-40	81
13:1-5	81-82
13:8	82
13:12-17	82
13:19-20	82-83
13:22	83
13:24-27	83
13:26	122
13:30-32	83
14:12-16	129, 130
14:29-31	123
14:54	123
14:61-62	117
14:66-72	123
15:39	117

accommodation of, 118
characteristic features of, 49
climax of, 115
community reflected by, 84-88, 116
discipleship in, 49
discontinuity between, 3:20 and 3:21 119
distinctive vocabulary of, 48-49
focus of, 131
insertion of Mark 9:9-13 125
intrusion into, 119
narrative feature of, 46-47
parables chapter of, 120
paradox of 8:35 123

narrative version of Q (QN). *(continued)*
  PN and, 36, 37, 48n24, 89, 117, 124, 131, 137-41, 161
  PN placed after, 136
  process joining passion account with, 34
  provenance of, 49-50
  teacher references in, 48, 58, 61, 72, 74, 76, 79, 81
  themes characteristic of, 102n27
narrative-critical study, 5
Neirynck, Frans, 41
Nero, 25-27, 30, 31, 137, 146
New Testament, 28, 138

Papias
  in agreement with Clement, 18
  on composition, 13n16
  conflicting testimony of, 21-24
  description of Mark's composition, 13n16
  on Mark and Peter, 30
  recap of, 20-21
  testimony of, 10-15, 16-17, 26, 27, 29, 36, 140, 145
  tradition not mentioned by, 28
parable(s), 150n6, 151
  chapter of QN, 120
  death of Jesus anticipated in, 131
  discourse, 156
  Jesus spoke in, 44, 56, 58, 67
  of Sower, 86-87, 120, 133
  of vineyard, 130, 131, 135
Passion Narrative (PN). *See also* Pre-Markan Passion Narrative

14:10-15:39	95
15:22	142, 143
15:34	142, 143
15:42	142, 143

  community reflected by Mark's earlier, 112-16
  compilation of, 145-46
  earlier, in Mark 14:1-15:46   103-12
  existence of, 6
  focus of, 96, 102n26
  motifs within, 49
  outline of, within Mark 14:1-16:8   94-96
  placement of QN before, 136
  Q without, 13n14
  QN and, 36, 37, 48n24, 89, 117, 124, 131, 137-41, 161
  synopsis of, 122
  teacher references in, 98, 104, 115

passion prediction
  at close of, 101
  Markan, 8:31   93, 94, 95, 99, 102, 112, 123, 127, 133
  Markan, 9:31   93, 95, 102, 112, 123, 127, 133
  Markan, 10:33–34   93, 94, 95, 99, 102, 112, 123, 127, 133
  as redactions, 136
  setting for, 125
  teaching of, 129
  within text of Mark, 126–28, 160
Passover, 97, 98, 103, 104, 112
patristic witness, 6, 9, 36, 37, 89
Paul
  as apostle, 22
  Christology reflected in Phil and, 102
  Corinthians writings from, 16
  letters of, 50
  mission in Corinth of, 34n46
  observation of, 124
  persecutions experienced by, 138
  during reign of Nero, 25
  in Rome, 23
  theology of, 90–91, 93, 137
  tradition of, in 1 Corinthians, 95, 101
Perrin, Norman, 161
persecution, 5, 24, 37, 136–38, 145
Peter
  acclamation of Jesus by, 122
  betrayal of, 133
  church role of, 153
  confrontation with Magus, 19, 144, 145, 146
  death of, 31
  denials of, 34
  departure from Rome by, 36–37
  failed discipleship of, 103, 123, 134
  First Epistle of, 30
  Gospel authorized by, 37
  Mark and, 11–21, 29–30, 36, 145, 146
  material from, 33, 34
  portrayal of, in Acts 1–10   146
  rehabilitation of, 103
  in Rome, 16, 21, 23, 25, 26
Philippians (Phil)
  2   92, 93, 96, 114
  2:8   113
  2:9–11   96
  9   92
  Christology reflected in Paul and, 102
  hymn in, 2   96, 135

Philo the Jew, 25, 29, 30, 32, 36
Pilate
  envy known by, 113, 114
  Jesus before, 100, 108–9, 134
  petition for body of Jesus to, 111
PN. *See* Passion Narrative
Pre-Markan Passion Narrative, 94
Proto-Mark Hypothesis, 6–7, 155–62
Psalm (Ps)
  22   114n28, 115, 134, 135
  22:1 in Mark 15:34   113
  118:26   129
  Jesus' suffering and death in, 139

Q. *See also* Mark without Q hypothesis (MwQH); narrative version of Q (QN)
  about, and content of, 39–41
  compilation of, 15
  existence of, 2n5, 6
  Luke and Matthew's dependence upon Mark and, 149
  Mark and, 41–43, 155
  narrative parallels between Mark and, 44–45
  without PN, 13n14
  reconstruction of, 89–90, 145
  sayings sequence by Luke, 40
  as stable tradition, 154
  textual parallels between Mark and, 43–44
  themes echoed of, 84
QN. *See* narrative version of Q

reader-response criticism, 3
redaction criticism, 2, 3, 39n3
religious leaders, Jewish, 85, 101, 113
rhetorical criticism, 4
Romans (Rom)
  5   93
  5:18–19   92, 96
  1 Corinthians aligned with, 92
Rome
  association of Mark's Gospel with, 137
  evidence of Gospel written in, 24–25, 36, 137
  Jews expelled from, 16, 19, 37, 138, 140, 145, 146
  Mark in, 9, 14, 19, 22, 37
  Neronian persecution in, 6
  Paul in, 23
  Peter in, 16, 21, 23, 25, 26
  Peter's departure from, 36–37

Rome (*continued*)
  request of brethren at, 30, 140, 145
  secretary to Pope Damasus in, 28
Sanhedrin, 116
Satan, 51, 56, 87, 115n30
Schmidt, Andreas, 42
Scripture(s)
  Christian canon of, 22
  for church reading, 19
  Hebrew, 84, 87
  interpretation of, 85
  Jewish, 84, 87, 130
Senior, Donald, 94
Septuagint, 50, 84, 87
seven veils, truth hidden by, 33, 34, 37
Smith, Morton, 32, 33
Solomon, 46, 47
Son of Man
  apocalyptic, 41
  appearance of, 84, 90, 123
  in Daniel 7   115
  eschatological, 136
  focus on, 103
  introduction to, 122
  Jesus as, 99, 141
  judgment by, 42, 49, 50, 93, 94, 131, 132, 139
  in Mark, 48n24
  in Markan passion predictions, 94, 95, 99, 102, 112, 123, 127, 133
  obedient, 96, 117
  references to suffering, 48n24
story criticism, 4
Streeter, Burnett H., 6n15
Strômateis (Clement), 33
Synoptic Gospels, 1, 156, 157, 159
Synoptic problem, 39n3, 40n6, 153
Synoptic relationships, 6n15, 39n5, 149, 152

Taylor, Vincent, 11, 22, 28, 31
teacher
  of God's kingdom, 7
  of God's will, 85, 93
  Jesus as, 40, 85n40, 90, 128
  PN references to, 98, 104, 115
  QN references to, 48, 58, 61, 72, 74, 76, 79, 81
Theodore, 20, 32, 33, 35n47, 36
Tuckett, Christopher M., 40n6, 41
the Twelve, 63n27, 74, 93n6, 99, 104, 121, 122, 142n3
Two-Document Hypothesis, 6n15, 39, 149, 153, 154, 155, 157, 161

Venetian tradition, 35–36

widow, 131, 133, 135, 136
Wisdom (Wis)
  2   49, 114
  7   46, 47, 49
Wisdom of Solomon
  background provided by, 46
  confidence of righteous in, 115
  as context for passion account, 114
  Jesus' suffering and death in, 139
  parallels to, 50, 144
  plan of unrighteous in, 119
woman
  anointing of, 102, 132, 133, 136
  as disciple, 101n25
  as follower of Jesus, 116
  reference to, 56, 61, 68, 82, 111
  in solidarity with progenitor, 91
  Syrophoenician, 88, 143
  will of God for, 90, 124

Zechariah (Zech)
  Jesus' suffering and death in, 139
  prophecy of, 13:7   99

www.ingramcontent.com/pod-product-compliance
Lightning Source LLC
Chambersburg PA
CBHW050140240426
43673CB00043B/1742